Best of Friends

Hilary Pereira

PRENTICE HALL LIFE

If life is what you make it, then making it better starts here.

What we learn today can change our lives tomorrow. It can change our goals or change our minds; open up new opportunities or simply inspire us to make a difference. That's why we have created a new breed of books that do more to help you make more of your life.

Whether you want more confidence or less stress, a new skill or a different perspective, we've designed *Prentice Hall Life* books to help you to make a change for the better. Together with our authors we share a commitment to bring you the brightest ideas and best ways to manage your life, work and wealth.

In these pages we hope you'll find the ideas you need for the life *you* want. Go on, help yourself.

It's what you make it

Best of Friends

How to help your child make friends
with confidence

Hilary Pereira

PEARSON

Prentice Hall

LIFE

Pearson Education Limited
Edinburgh Gate
Harlow
Essex CM20 2JE
England

ISBN: 978-0-273-71430-9
Commissioning Editor: Emma Shackleton
Project Editor: Helena Caldon
Designer: Annette Peppis
Cover Design: R&D&Co
Production Controller: Franco Forgione

Printed and bound by Henry Ling, UK

The Publisher's policy is to use paper manufactured from sustainable forests.

Contents

For my sister and dearest friend, Vanessa, and her family.
And for my closest friends: you know who you are.

'The better part of one's life consists of his friendships.'
ABRAHAM LINCOLN, 16TH PRESIDENT OF THE USA

Introduction

My mother used to say 'There's no friend like an old friend', and how true this seems to be as life goes on! I remember clearly my first day at primary school when, distraught at being separated from my mum, I looked up to see a friendly, sunny face and hear its five-year-old owner announce: 'Don't worry, I'll take care of you'. She was true to her word and to this day she remains my oldest friend – and someone to whom I am still so close that I count her as family.

My secondary school experience was also enhanced greatly by a circle of five good friends – all of whom are still an integral part of my life and each other's, even though we have each chosen to tread quite different paths. Maintaining close contact with mates who have seen you through your schooldays; teen rebellion; family crises; first romances; questionable fashion choices; bad haircuts; wedding nerves; new parenthood and much, much more means that they are the ones who know you best, and who can help you put things into perspective when your memory of events, people and places may have become a bit skewed.

Friendships formed in childhood can have a very far-reaching effect, inasmuch as they endow us with feelings of security and confidence from a young age that can be long-lasting. This in turn encourages us to socialize and bond with our peers from babyhood onwards, and this can be terrifically rewarding in terms of building self-esteem, as well as providing plenty of playmates. The ability to maintain friendships successfully also involves learning to share, to consider others and to behave democratically – all of which are important life skills.

But how can we ensure that our own children are indeed self-assured enough to form friendships in the first place? Can we have any control over which children they bond with? What if a friendship seems to be more destructive than nurturing? Suppose acute shyness seems to be leading to isolation and insecurity?

Many aspects of parenting leave us full of self-doubt, wondering if we're taking the right course and doing the right thing – and this is certainly true when it comes to building our children's confidence and helping them to make friends. This book aims to offer plenty of sound advice that will help you encourage your child to form early, enduring bonds and to socialize confidently. There are also lots of 'quick fixes' that will help you deal with crises of confidence, as well as undesirable behaviour (if these issues are spotted in their early stages), as well as simple, but effective, longer-term strategies for building your child's self-esteem and encouraging independence.

Raising well-rounded children is not only about teaching them right from wrong, but also about instilling in them a sense of citizenship, community, responsibility and consideration – all of which will enable them to form the kind of lifelong friendships that have certainly helped to shape my life for the better.

Hilary Pereira

Author's note: In this book I have elected to refer to children alternately as 'he' or 'she' from chapter to chapter. This avoids the rather clumsy 'him/her', 'his/her' and 'he/she' options. Where advice is more pertinent to one gender than the other, I have attempted to make this clear within the text. For the same reason, I have also referred to parents mainly as 'mum', although these references are entirely interchangeable with 'dad', except where obviously targeted at one or the other.

The relationship between confidence and friendship

Can you imagine being dumped at a crowded party where you know no one, and being told that you must strike up at least one new friendship before you leave? Unless you are a relatively self-confident person, such a suggestion would probably leave you feeling at best uncomfortable and, at worst, like running for the hills.

And yet this is what we sometimes expect of our young children. True, they are typically pretty uninhibited and non-judgemental in their earliest days – and this undoubtedly makes such situations less awkward for them – but if they have never been taught how to begin to relate to their peers, being faced with a room full of strangers can be just as daunting for them as for adults.

A prerequisite of being able to reach out to others is having a sense of self-worth; for babies and young children this must be instilled in them by their parents. Self-worth is linked to self-image – how we see ourselves. This personal insight comes largely from early experiences, environment, family, teachers, society and friends – all external factors that we as parents need to ensure are nurturing and supportive. Once a baby or child feels confident and secure, he can then begin to appreciate the worth of others. This is why friendship and confidence go hand in hand.

No one is born confident; confidence is something that has to be learned – and it is through feeling loved, appreciated and respected that confidence blossoms and grows.

How important is confidence in our lives?

The value of feeling liked, accepted and respected for who we are is immeasurable and is one of life's great motivators; it also lies at the heart of confidence. However, for young children it is the feeling of approval that's most affirming, and this is why it's so important that we, as parents, offer encouragement and praise whenever it is due.

Think back to your earliest memories of doing something new – perhaps riding a bike or holding a pencil properly. Did you feel anxious at first? Were these feelings of anxiety heightened or assuaged by whoever who was teaching you? If you were given messages such as: 'No, not like that. Stop. You haven't been watching properly', the chances are that your confidence took a knock and you felt discouraged. However, if you were told: 'Well done, that's a great first attempt, now let's try it again', you probably felt yourself growing in confidence and trusting in your own ability.

Self-confidence is a great spur to most people, pushing them towards attainment and then on to greater achievement – whatever they are attempting. As one education consultant put it, a child with self-confidence 'will have retained a natural curiosity for learning and will be eager and enthusiastic when presented with a new challenge'. Expecting to be liked (even admired) and approved of is another great starting point for being able to relate to other people: after all, if you already feel that you are likeable and worthwhile as a person, why would anyone want to treat

you otherwise? True, not all attempts at friendship work out – and knocks to self-esteem are an inevitable part of rejection – but having the confidence to try is a wonderful foundation.

Why are friendships important?

Friendships, especially those that are enduring, are affirming at all ages and represent the ongoing approval of ourselves as people. For children, friendships provide a separate source of validation from the affirmation of unconditional love that comes from their parents and so they are, in some senses, just as important to them. At times your child's friends will have the power to make him really happy; at others absolutely miserable; however, in either situation it is to his peers that he will often turn for feedback and advice, because it is to them that he can best relate.

It has been proven that friendships are crucial to self-esteem and that they also provide children with a yardstick by which to measure themselves: through friendships they can compare themselves with their peers; share the day-to-day pleasures and frustrations of childhood with others of a similar age, and also build a sense of empathy and camaraderie.

For pre-schoolers, friends serve several important purposes: they offer a sense of security in unfamiliar settings, such as nursery or playgroup; they are companions,

One long-term international research study, published in 1998, showed that children who had a close friend at age 11 had a greater sense of self-worth when they were adults than those who did not, and were also less likely to suffer from depression in the long term.

playmates and, in some cases, leaders in games and other activities; they provide a gateway to a social life for your child; and they reinforce a sense of separateness from you which will in turn help your child to become more independent. Your young child won't, of course, be able to appreciate or understand fully the importance of friendship in his early years, but he will almost certainly respond to it. If his best friend, or a group of friends, suddenly rejects him – as frequently happens, especially in children of primary-school age – he may feel worthless and demotivated for a time. However, when his friendships are strong and consistent, or when he is included in a new group situation, he will feel happier, more confident, more self-assured and better motivated.

By the time a child enters junior school he will have had greater experience of how friendships can and do fluctuate and change, but this doesn't mean that the path is any smoother for him. Whilst he may be better equipped to react and respond to upsets within his social group, he will still be very vulnerable to others' opinions of him – particularly those of his peers – and his performance at school and general happiness may come under threat if an

unhappy situation is ongoing. This is all tied up with another role that friendship plays – that of allowing your child to compare himself, favourably or otherwise, with others, and vice versa. (Advice on helping your child to resolve ongoing problems, as well as how to spot and combat bullying, is offered in later chapters.)

Constancy in friendships is just one factor that influences how effectively the relationship will bolster a child's self-esteem; another is the approval of his parents. This approval is easily and gladly given when the social group seems to conform to the parents' idea of who is a 'suitable' friend for their child, but can be more reticently offered when parents don't wholeheartedly rubber stamp a child's friend or friends.

What are friendships for?

There are four main functions that friendships fulfil:

○ They encourage children to acquire and build on the social skills needed to form longer-term relationships, specifically cooperation and reciprocity.

○ They provide important emotional resources, both in terms of enjoyment and comfort.

○ They allow children a framework within which to learn about themselves and others.

○ They can be templates for the relationships children will create in later life.

Always remember that childhood is a time of emotional as well as physical upheaval in which many changes inevitably occur, from switching schools to moving house and generally growing up. It also involves experiencing a variety of very public successes and failures at school, such as excelling in coursework, or failing to be chosen as a key player in a particular sport. Throughout all this, if a child has the constancy of established friendships he will fare much better. Like a ship anchored firmly at sea, he may feel buffeted by the storms of childhood, but he will benefit from the ongoing support of strong bonds with his peers.

What friendship means at different ages

In young children it's not so much individual friends who provide feelings of security and continuity: it's inclusion, companionship and a sense of belonging, all of which result in confidence. Sometimes a toddler might recruit a peer as his 'friend' purely because the child owns a toy he fancies playing with! Up to the age of three, children are usually extremely egocentric and largely unconcerned about the feelings and wellbeing of others. Even after their third birthdays, it can take months or even years for them to realize that theirs aren't the only needs deserving consideration. So don't expect too much too young: this self-centredness is a perfectly normal stage of development (and, let's face it, something some people never grow out of!).

Because your young child's main concerns will tend to be for himself rather than others, it's often no great cause for concern if a favourite playmate leaves the area; or if the pair of them have a falling out; or if you and the other child's mum drift apart, as almost every other child in his circle is a potential replacement. This is just as well, because sometimes the pre- and post-baby friendships we mothers make are founded first and foremost on the need to go through the same experiences together, so they can be quickly outgrown once we are fully-fledged, confident parents and no longer in need of such a strong support group.

The early associations your baby or toddler enjoys are just as important in terms of his social development as the more lasting friendships that he will form later.

Once a child starts school, at around age four, friendships may still be made, broken, remade or finally abandoned in favour of new alliances. This is perfectly normal; children like to explore each other's personalities, grow in confidence and discover the companions who suit them best. You may be surprised to find that your child forges close ties with another child who seems his polar opposite in terms of personality, but it's a common occurrence. Just as some children bond best with others who think, feel and behave as they do, many are attracted to those who display characteristics that they themselves lack. Studies show that girls of this age tend to form closer attachments to select groups of other girls than boys do with other boys; boys tend to widen the net of friendship and play in larger, more random groups.

By junior-school age, children have often made the friends they will keep until high school. At this stage the experimentation with different personalities is largely over as they develop a need for more lasting friendships. Relationships – particularly those between girls – become crucial to them, and girls start to judge themselves more and more by the attitudes of others towards them, and less and less by parental approval. It's no coincidence that over the past eight or so years, researchers have discovered that 'pre-teen' hormonal activity amongst girls begins from around age eight. In boys it typically kicks in from around age 13.

In both sexes, a kind of 'herd mentality' may begin to emerge at this stage, where groups of children show allegiance to particular media influences, such as Bratz; a professional football club; a popular children's TV channel or a superhero character. Children will commonly use their own coded language around now to communicate within the group: this is specifically designed to include certain individuals and exclude others (including you!).

It is also a stage at which confidence can take a knock, as children are vulnerable to rejection if they don't go along with the crowd. You can help prevent this by encouraging your child to be confident in his own views and his individuality, or at least do some damage limitation if the crisis has already occurred. (This is explored in detail in Chapter 4.)

School Year 7 can be seminal in the formation of long-lasting friendships. This is the time when your child makes the transition from junior school to high school, and you may find that your child's preference for one establishment over another may be more to do with who else is going there than whether the facilities are likely to play to his strengths.

This stage involves great change and emotional upheaval for both boys and girls and, as discussed above, the support of close friendship may be crucial to how well a child settles. There is, of course, plenty of scope in this first year for making new friends, and this could be your opportunity to try again to exert fresh influence over your child's choices. So discuss with him the qualities that are most desirable in friends – empathy, kindness, generosity, and so on – and encourage him to look for these characteristics when he's making new friends. You may also want to discuss emerging friendships with his teacher, especially now that your contact with the school is likely to be far less 'hands on' than when he was still in junior school; the staff need to be your eyes and ears at this crucial time.

Changing patterns of friendship

The patterns of friendship cannot be seen in a prescriptive way – particularly as different outside influences, children's characters and personal styles will play an important role in each individual case. Scientists, educationalists and parents have, however, made some general observations about how

Confidence and relationships from birth to age 11

Here's a little insight into how children typically develop the ability to relate to themselves, and others, throughout childhood:

6 months   Your baby will make regular eye contact with his main carers and will smile and babble to make social contact.

12 months   He will show a preference for familiar people and begin to take an interest in other children.

2 years   Your toddler will make more demands for attention. He will start to defend his own possessions but also begin to play alongside his peers.

5 years   He will become more interested in other children's activities, will show affection for his siblings and will engage in simple games with his peers.

8 years   Your child will form strong friendships, preferring some children over others. He will start to challenge your authority – if he hasn't already started to do so!

9–11 years He will enjoy spending more time with friends and having sleepovers, cooperate in team games and teamwork and show more of an interest in the opposite sex.

the emphasis on the interaction between children tends to shift as they grow. Little children, for instance, frequently use friendship as a bargaining tool. 'I'll be your best friend'; 'We won't play with you unless…'; 'I'm telling on you' are all commonly heard phrases amongst children of infant-school age and younger. You could say that it's a form of emotional blackmail – but without the intent! To these youngsters, especially the more dominant personalities, the promise of friendship – or its withdrawal – is used as a way of wheedling certain behaviour out of their peers. Ironically, this is also the age group where the majority of children are unequipped to forge their own way and assert their own preferences, especially if these go against the grain of their peers.

Confidence plays a large role here, too: the child who issues the threat appears to be more confident than the assenting child, who may seem to lack self-assurance. Often, though, it is the other way round: the child who is the protagonist may, in fact, need the reassurance that his views are important enough to withstand his threat, while the child who goes along with these views may have enough confidence to put his own beliefs to one side for now.

Try to find some time to discuss these issues with your child: use the chat as an opportunity to talk about the power of friendships, and how controlling one child or a group of individuals can be. The upside of this, of course, is that your child will also learn to feel a real sense of positive control if he sticks to his principles in the face of pressure from others.

At junior school, personal preferences and a sense of individuality tend to emerge, along with, if you're lucky, a drive to seek the approval of adults. These children are often less likely to go along with the wishes of others and are more influenced by the attitudes of parents, teachers and other authority figures. For them, friendship is a welcome and necessary support, but it is no longer as influential as it once was.

This is also the age, though, when manipulation and bullying commonly start, as children begin to realize the role of power and control and how these characteristics can often get them what they want. If you think your child is going along with the bad behaviour or attitudes of others, it's worth probing further to find out why he is doing this, and if he is being threatened or otherwise abused by his peers in any way.

By high school, the primary influence when it comes to choosing friends is fashion. This is the age when children may break off into splinter groups or even 'gangs'. Groups of pre-teens and teens often all dress in a kind of 'teen uniform', and will probably shun peers who are not following the same trends. Music and other media preferences tend to converge during this period, and much of the focus of pre-teens is on 'the scene' of the moment. This age group may also latch on to perceived social injustices, animal rights – or some other cause their family doesn't support. This is usually an attempt to reinforce their individuality, although, again, herd mentality often follows. It's not

uncommon for children who last night happily tucked into chilli con carne to announce they are sworn vegetarians the next – leaving those who haven't made the same decision being ousted (however temporarily) from the group!

Parental approval is often regarded as highly undesirable at this age, so you may find anarchic tendencies of varying degrees emerging. This is a common period for crises of confidence to occur – and whilst your child may appear to be standing up for his beliefs, he may actually be going along with the crowd because he lacks the confidence to stand against it. At this stage of a child's development the wish to be part of a group accompanies the need for a common identity and sense of belonging, so it's important for his self-esteem that you take his feelings seriously.

All boys – or girls – together?

Childhood pairings and strong friendships do tend to emerge from within same-gender groups, with girls mostly teaming up with other girls, and boys sticking together. Sometimes you see strong bonds being forged between a girl and a boy, but this is more to do with personality attraction than with gender. (Often in these boy/girl friendships either the boy will be more 'feminine' or the girl will be more 'tomboyish' than usual.) Shared interests are the main influential factor in childhood relationships, and this is why the same-gender groups tend to form.

The friendless child

An apparently friendless child – or a child with few friends – isn't necessarily unhappy or lonely, although if your own child is in this situation it is, of course, important that you find out whether or not this is the case. 'Children have different needs; some like to have a large group of friends, whilst others feel happier with a few closer friends or, in less usual situations, seem to have no friends to speak of,' says child psychologist Laverne Antrobus. 'As a parent, it's up to you to check out where your child places having friends in his hierarchy of needs: maybe it's of little importance to him and he's fairly self-sufficient, in which case you have no need to worry immediately. You may discover, however, that your child is indeed feeling very lonely – and this may translate for him into feeling unwanted, less desirable than other children, or even unlikeable. The message that you want to give your child is that having friends is a good thing. Talk to him about the support that you gain from your own friends, why you have chosen them and how it feels to have someone outside of the family in whom you can confide and trust.'

Imaginary friends

It's very common for young children to have imaginary friends – and it is considered by some child behaviour experts to be a very healthy development. Imaginary friends are the products of fertile imaginations, and one US study found that 65 per cent of children had an imaginary

friend by the age of seven. A UK study into the developmental effects of having an imaginary companion (IC) is still underway at the time of writing, but early results suggest that the IC children have an intellectual advantage in terms of perspective-taking – and that this correlation appears to be due to the fact that these children engage in large amounts of pretend play, which in turn has a positive effect on many developmental milestones.

Sometimes an imaginary friend will come to the fore whenever the child himself is bored or lonely and is away from other children; sometimes they seem to accompany children everywhere. These pretend friendships can fulfil some very important needs: a child may, for instance, confide in or confess to his imaginary friend, and this can help to alleviate feelings of guilt or anxiety. Talking to an imaginary friend may even enable him to 'rehearse' something he wants to tell you; he knows his 'friend' will not interrupt him or argue back (unless he makes this happen); he can even blame his friend when things go wrong, and this special imaginary ally provides an outlet for any emotion he may otherwise find difficult to express.

For some children, an imaginary friend is a kind of alter ego: a very shy child may, for instance, have a boisterous imaginary friend; a confident, outgoing child may devise someone who is timid and needs looking after. In some cases this sort of friendship offers a child the opportunity to explore behaviours they wouldn't otherwise display. An only child can find imaginary friendships particularly fulfilling, and may hang on to them for longer than a child with siblings might.

Generally, there's no need to be concerned about an imaginary friend. Usually a child will know his friend is not real and will outgrow the need for this 'relationship' – but it's a process that can't be rushed, so let your child set his own pace. It will help if you humour your child, joining in with the pretence when he wants you to, but allowing him his privacy when he doesn't.

Tempting though it may be to tease your child, never make fun of his association with his imaginary friend or try to control the friend, but let him know you're aware this person isn't real. Do this by saying something encouraging at the same time, such as 'It's lovely to pretend you have another friend whenever you feel like it, isn't it?'.

It's also okay to enter into the game once your child realizes that you are pretending along with him, and this can be useful in helping to unravel emotional difficulties. If, for example, the imaginary friend is crying because someone has been unkind to him, it could be that your child is re-enacting a scene from the school playground that involved him. In this case, you could advise the imaginary friend to confide in his mum or tell a teacher what's been happening. You could then say to your child, 'I'm sure that's what you would do if you were in your friend's place, wouldn't you?'. In this way you're able to impart advice indirectly without your child having to admit to his own feelings if this makes him feel uncomfortable.

Instances when it would be wise to seek professional advice about a child's relationship with his imaginary friend are: if it becomes destructive, if your child is too reliant on it or if it prevents him from making actual friendships, in which case you should talk to your doctor or health visitor about a referral to a child behaviour therapist.

Friendship and the only child

Whilst imaginary friends can be invaluable to only children, a lone child's real core friendships – and those of children who have much older or younger siblings – may be more important to him than they would be to a child who has siblings who are close in age to him. Your child may, for instance, regard his best friend as a sibling substitute, and there's nothing wrong with this degree of closeness, as long as the other child is happy to reciprocate. You can encourage this bond by inviting the other child for sleepovers and weekend visits, so that your child experiences the pleasure of sharing his free time with someone of, or around, his own age.

Of course, you may find that your child experiences some of the same spats with his close friend that he might have done with a sibling but, again, this is perfectly normal; just ensure that they make up quickly, as would happen if he had a brother or sister living with him, rather than letting the dispute drag on.

That said, it's also a good idea to encourage a range of friendships from different sources, so that if your child does have a permanent falling-out with his best mate – or if he loses contact for some other reason – he has other good friendships to fall back on. Make an effort to keep early friendships going, even after your child starts school. For instance, did you make a special friend in your antenatal or postnatal group whose child was born at the same time? Try to maintain this relationship by meeting up, say, once a month. Also, encourage your child to make friends with children at any of the out-of-school groups he attends. You can facilitate this by asking both the child and his mum back for tea or out for a picnic lunch.

The more friends your child makes from his different resources, the less alone he will feel when he is without peer company at home.

Don't forget, too, that a lot of only children really cherish the extra attention they get from their parents and the time they spend together as a family. These children also get to mix with more adults than other children, so they can gain perspectives that other children won't have, giving them a broader social experience.

'Only' doesn't have to mean 'lonely' – as long as your child is exposed to as rich a social life as he will enjoy.

Parental influence

The argument of whether a child's development is influenced more by nature or nurture is a perennial favourite – and one which is never likely to be resolved fully. It is generally agreed, however, that children's behaviour can be influenced enormously by their parents or other main carers. How often, for instance, have you heard your child scolding his toys in the same way that you have scolded him? Are you confident that, just as he says 'please' and 'thank you' in your home, he automatically does the same when visiting friends' homes? Does he deal with frustration or disappointment in the same way as either you or your partner? If you can answer yes to these questions, it will be clear to you that the way you behave yourself has a direct influence on how your child responds in given situations.

In the early days, too, your child will be eager to please you, and this will be his motivation for good behaviour and positive interaction with other children. If he does display antisocial behaviour (which most young children will, from time to time), he will probably respond to your guidance on how a different approach might produce a more positive result. Later, however, as he develops different moral reasons for cooperation, he may not be so conducive to changing his behaviour to impress you. This, again, is a perfectly normal stage of development, and one which is borne out of a move towards self-reliance (see pages 86–7 for more on this).

Action plan

How to set a great example

The way in which you yourself treat strangers, friends and acquaintances will impact on how your child chooses and conducts his peer relationships. You can have positive influence, too, in the way that you interact with your partner and other family members – and it's good to get across the message that family members are also your friends, and that you are able to accommodate their behaviour. This is particularly effective if you have views that differ from those of your relatives, yet still maintain a good relationship: it teaches your children to respect and even celebrate others' differences.

Children are quick to recognize acts of kindness and generosity, so help your child to learn in a positive way about making friends by setting an example yourself:

o If a new neighbour moves in down the road, let your child see you popping by with a welcome card and spending a few minutes chatting. (Even if you are normally shy or reticent, it's a good idea to allow him to see that you are confident enough to approach a stranger kindly.)

o If the newcomer has children, find ways that you and your child can welcome them: if their children are younger, perhaps you could pass on some toys he has outgrown.

o If another child's parent seems to be going through a stressful period, offer whatever help you can, and let your child see what you're doing. Again, this may not come entirely naturally to you, but in the same way that your child

will learn to adopt your fears and anxieties, he is also likely to approach other situations with confidence if you do. In this way, he'll learn that he can take the initiative by starting conversations with unfamiliar children, and he'll begin to see the value of setting aside time to help others.

○ If you fall out with your partner or relative, let your child witness you apologizing and making up. Show him that you can take it in turns to listen to each other's point of view calmly and without shouting before coming to a resolution that suits you both and shaking hands or exchanging a kiss (however hard this may seem!). He needs to feel confident that it's perfectly normal to have disagreements and squabbles sometimes, but equally that he doesn't have to lose face when making things right and that normality can be restored quickly and without recriminations. Indeed, this is what lasting friendship is all about.

○ Behave like a friend towards your child, as well as a parent: tell him how much you like him (as well as love him) and spend time playing games of his choosing. Don't make comparisons between him and his friends or siblings; let him know that you like and love him for who he is.

○ When he does something to disappoint or anger you, try to criticize the behaviour rather than the child. Say 'I really don't like rudeness' rather than 'You are a very rude boy'. Imposing a negative label on your child will lower his self-esteem, and he may even continue to behave in the same negative way because he learns that this is what you expect of him.

What parents say about friendships

'My own parents were clearly best friends as well as partners, and their influence has undoubtedly helped me to form lasting friendships. Both Mum and Dad would always consider each other before making even the most minor decision: Mum wouldn't cook the dinner until Dad had agreed that it was something he fancied, and Dad wouldn't just turn the TV over to the sports channel if there was something Mum wanted to watch first. These little gestures of kindness and consideration have really influenced the way I interact with my own partner and family. As a result I never knowingly make a decision that could affect someone else adversely without discussing it with them first.'

ADRIENNE, 34, FROM COLDHARBOUR, MUM TO LEWIS, 3, AND DONNY, 1

'I think parents are the most influential role models that their children will ever have, and when it comes to valuing people as friends, my partner Gary and I try to make sure that my son and daughter will share this view. We make a point of remembering friends' birthdays, celebrating their successes and reminding them why we like them, and we've overheard both our children doing the same with their best friends, which is great!'

LOUISA, 37, FROM LONDON, MUM TO ALEX, 10, AND REBECCA, 7

'Lydia used to be such a shy child but suddenly, at age 5, when she was in Year 1, she started taking an interest in how other children felt about things. She came home on several occasions telling me how one child had hurt another's feelings, or how she had taken a little friend to the school office after they'd had a fall in the playground. Now she has many friends and gets lots of invitations to play. Her teacher tells me she's a popular child, and I'm sure it's because she cares about others. I'm really hoping Paolo will turn out the same way, but it's a bit early to tell yet.'

ANGELINA, 29, FROM LEITH, MUM TO LYDIA, 7, AND PAOLO, 2

'Because we have four children who are close in age, they've always been used to having to share and take turns, so when friends come round there's never been much of a problem – everyone just mucks in. Sometimes a visiting child will become a bit possessive about one of his or her toys, and our children can't understand it at all. In the end, I think as long as parents are aware of how their children are interacting with others, social skills do tend to develop with age – it's just that ours have had to learn the arts of diplomacy and democracy a bit sooner than most!'

LIAM , 31, FROM BELFAST, DAD TO JOE, 6, LIZZIE, 5, AND TWINS CAITLIN AND CALLUM, 3

'The mates I made in the first year of high school, when I was just 11, are still amongst my closest friends now. I think there's a lot to be said for going through rites of passage

together and knowing a person's past: you're not family, so you're not going to leap to a judgement as quickly as a relative might, but you can help each other to be objective when dealing with problems and crises of confidence. It's my hope that even if my two children go on to university, they'll make lasting friendships while they are at school, too. I don't think there's any substitute for friendships made in childhood.'

ANGELICA BROUGHTON, 36, FROM CORNWALL, MUM TO ALICIA, 10, AND KATIE, 7

How to build your child's confidence

Building confidence in our children should become a way of life once we become parents – and the great news is that you can begin practically from day one. First, though, it may be helpful to explore all the different definitions of 'confidence'.

What is confidence?

Common terms most readily associated with the word 'confidence' are self-belief, self-reliance and assurance. In fact, confidence could be described as the opposite of fear or timidity. When applied to a baby, the word 'confident' usually suggests that she is happy to be passed from person to person; that she doesn't immediately cry when approached by a stranger or that she is willing to try new tastes and textures. When this term is used in relation to a child, confident can mean that she seems happy in her own skin; assured of her own abilities; outgoing; chatty or ready to take risks.

Babies and children are not born with an innate sense of confidence: it's something that has to be learnt – and this is why it's so important that we, as parents, learn the skills to imbue our children with confidence right from the start. It's also why those children with parents who neglect to focus on the positive aspects of their development and behaviour very often end up being needy, self-critical and emotionally repressed young people and adults. It's all too easy to criticize and correct our children – thinking that this is what teaching them is all about – but it doesn't always come as naturally to praise, encourage or even notice their small achievements, and this is the key to raising truly confident children who have the skills to relate to others positively.

Feel the fear

In order to appreciate the importance of our role in building a sense of confidence in our children from an early age, it's helpful to try to imagine how vulnerable a newborn must feel when entering the world. Imagine, for instance, that you suddenly find yourself thrust into a place where you have absolutely no knowledge or experience of the language, customs, accepted behaviours, etiquette or geography. Perhaps you've been sent on a reconnaissance trip by your boss: he will be seriously displeased if you fail to fit in, but he hasn't provided you with a guide. How scary will it be to step off the plane into the unknown? It hardly bears thinking about! On the other hand, let's say you are provided not only with a guide, but also with a translator and an expert in the dos and don'ts of the culture or an ex-pat who has been living the lifestyle for years before your arrival. Given this situation, how much more willing will you be to try to overcome obstacles? How instrumental will these individuals be in helping you to build your confidence during your stay?

If you now relate this scenario to your baby or young child (where you and your partner are the experienced guides

and your child is the wary traveller), it's easy to see how being shown what to do in a supportive and encouraging way is a crucial factor in building confidence and feelings of self-esteem. It's particularly helpful to visualize such a scene when you're dealing with a child who seems to be finding it hard to gain confidence, despite all your efforts.

Confidence tricks

Right from birth you can help to build your baby's confidence, both with practical exercises and in everyday life. The ways and means may change and develop with your child, but the principles will remain largely the same.

Action plan
Birth and early days
○ Keep her feeling safe and secure by cuddling, swaddling and picking her up whenever she needs comforting.

○ Provide a cosy, tranquil environment for when she's sleepy (although don't tiptoe around her or you will be making a rod for your own back later on when she is unable to sleep in anything but silence).

○ Chat to her often: babies have been proven to recognize their mothers' voices from their time spent in the womb, so she will feel reassured by the familiar tones.

○ Use her name as well as your own – and that of anyone else with whom she has frequent contact. She'll quickly learn to recognize names.

o Settle her into a routine as early on as you can (athough do let her lead the way). Set consistent feed times where possible (but feed on demand in the very early days); regular nap or rest times; a bath and final feed before you put her down for the night, and so on. Babies and young children find great security in such rituals and routines.

o Sing and talk to her in soothing, gentle tones. Even though babies don't actually understand vocabulary, they are very much attuned to recognizing tones of voice and inflections.

o Resist the urge to try to force your baby to be confident by passing her from person to person – especially if she seems at all nervous or unsettled. In the early days, restrict physical handling to two or three key people who she will recognize and form bonds with. It will be enough for her to get used to other people's voices before she feels comfortable being cuddled and held by them.

o It is possible to over-handle a baby, so teach yourself to recognize the times when she is crying because she is over-stimulated. Let her have some peaceful time without being held if she enjoys this; even if she doesn't sleep, she may be happy just playing with her toes and having a look around her. You can use this as an opportunity to help your baby develop a 'healthy separation' from you; she will become confident and secure knowing that you are close by, so she will not feel the need to be physically held.

Action plan

Settled babies (3–6 months)

Once your baby is settled in to her home and routine you can build on the confidence she has gained. Try some or all of the following:

○ Share the care with your partner or other responsible adult or older child – but encourage them to stick to your routine as far as possible so your baby won't feel too much is changing.

○ Introduce new sights and sounds by bringing visitors into the house and taking her out and about more.

○ Join a mother-and-baby group, if you don't already belong to one.

○ Repeat familiar songs and games with her: she'll gain confidence just by recognizing tunes or patterns.

○ Give her a baby-safe area to explore and play in. Once she is able to sit supported you can dangle ribbons or favourite toys for her to reach out and swipe at, or place objects just out of comfortable reach so that she will lean forward to retrieve them.

○ Once she is able to sit up unsupported, let her experience the freedom of a door bouncer: she will love the feeling that she is able to control her own movements, as well as the exhilaration of bouncing around and the new perspective she'll gain from being upright. However, do read and follow the manufacturer's instructions carefully.

○ Praise all attempts at something new – in fact, praise your baby in general. Self-esteem comes primarily from the approval of those closest to us, and you can't spoil a baby of this age with too much praise or positive attention.

Action plan
Older babies (6–12 months)

o Chat to your baby, whether you're playing with her or working near her, and listen for her babbling responses: she may try to emulate your tone of voice, make little sounds of her own or giggle back at you. Feeling that she is being listened to will help build her self-esteem, so by talking back to her she will experience the pleasure of 'conversation'!

o When she is able to do a few things for herself – like putting finger foods into her mouth, reaching for her toys or completing a simple puzzle – encourage her to do it again and again. The more proficient she becomes at things, the more confident she'll grow – and she'll love repeating things she's good at already.

o Let your baby take the lead and don't be over-ambitious for her: getting her to try things before she's ready will just set her up for failure. Provide her with lots of stimulating, age-appropriate things to play with. They don't need to cost a lot of money, especially if you borrow them from a toy library or swap with friends.

o Set aside time each day to play and interact with your baby. Make sure you don't get distracted and then she will feel that you are really devoting your time to her. Encourage your partner and other people who play a regular part in her life to do the same.

○ It's never too early to make your home safe for a more mobile baby, especially once she starts crawling or 'cruising' (pulling herself up to standing and holding on to furniture as she navigates her way around the room). Put protective cushion pads on sharp corners of tables, shelves, coffee tables and any other furniture your child might bump in to; tidy away any cables or leads; put stops on doors and cupboards to prevent exploring fingers becoming trapped; position breakables well out of reach and ensure that there are no dangerous items such as pen tops, paperclips, batteries or other small objects lying on the floor.

○ Praise your baby often.

Action plan

Toddlers and pre-schoolers

○ Ignore as many as possible of the less desirable episodes and outbursts typical of this age range, and continue to heap praise on your child for any good behaviour! Not only will she realize that she can gain positive attention and other rewards when she pleases you, she'll also remain secure in the knowledge that her worst behaviour will not deprive her of your love.

○ Brief family, friends and anyone who looks after your child about your strategies for dealing with unacceptable behaviour so that it is handled consistently by everyone. Your child will feel more secure if she knows that the rules are always the same regarding behaviour, no matter whose care she is in at the time.

○ Allow her greater independence where possible. After all, what does it matter if she spends several days on the trot wearing the same dressing-up outfit? The important thing is that she's had the freedom to choose for herself.

○ Introduce new skills to your child – particularly those that will enhance the role-play games that children of this age tend to love. No-cook cookery (such as basic sandwich making, decorating plain biscuits and helping to mix a salad together); a little cleaning and sweeping with her own brush and duster; playing with toy tool boxes; digging in the garden or watering plants with child-size equipment will all reinforce the fact that you think she's a helpful and capable member of the family.

○ Give your child plenty of opportunities to build on skills she's already good at: her confidence will blossom by knowing that she can climb; tumble; swim; run; skip; dance; ride trikes or bikes; paint or build stuff in a secure environment. All these skills can be practised and improved upon, which will boost her self-esteem even further.

○ Give her a few special responsibilities of her own (but do supervize wherever you feel it is necessary): let her feed the hamster; fetch her own drinking cup; take her bowl and spoon out to the kitchen after breakfast; choose a bedtime storybook; make a first attempt at cleaning her own teeth (although you'll need to check and re-brush until she's around seven, as she simply won't have the necessary dexterity before then).

○ Praise your child whenever the opportunity arises.

Action plan

School-age children

○ Because many children start school shortly after their fourth birthday, the younger children in reception classes may have similar abilities and attitudes to pre-schoolers, so if this is the case for your child, follow the tips on the previous page for this age group, too.

○ Respond to your child's interest in learning by providing her with opportunities to practise reading, number work and letter formation – once you know the methods being taught at school. She will thrive on the extra attention and, as long as she enjoys her schoolwork, she will gain in confidence the more she understands.

○ When formal homework is introduced, sit quietly with your child and support her. It's no good doing it for her or telling her all the answers unless she understands it, as this will result in a loss of confidence when she can't replicate the work in class. Encourage her, help her to work things out for herself and show her how to present her work neatly. If you feel that she is struggling, abandon the work after ten minutes or so and put a note in her bag for her teacher to let her know what happened.

○ Give your child a voice in your household: ask for her suggestions for what you could do as a family at the weekend; get her opinion on the meals you cook for her; involve her in general conversations where appropriate (and where the subject matter is not appropriate, try to avoid having such discussions within her earshot); give her some choices as to how she could spend the last few minutes of her evening once her normal routine is complete and she's ready to hop into bed. Would she like a story with you? A quiet game of cards? A cuddle and a chat?

○ If you have older children, do give your younger child the chance to contribute to family discussions, too. Often we disregard unwittingly the opinions of the youngest member of the family and there can be a tendency to keep them as babies for as long as possible; in such cases we may turn a blind eye to how much they are maturing.

○ Spend one-to-one time with your child each day so that she feels valued and cared for. Chat about your day and hers, and ask her open questions that encourage dialogue, such as 'What can you tell me about your day?', rather than closed questions which invite a yes/no answer, such as 'Did you have a good day?'.

○ Introduce your child to new, age-appropriate skills such as bike-riding, climbing, in-line skating or karate. It's always tempting to keep your child away from all potentially dangerous activities, but as long as you ensure that you are teaching her to follow the proper safety procedures or are enrolling her in a reputable class, adding extra skills like these will not only mean that she will increase her physical confidence, but that she'll also gain in self-esteem from the kudos that mastering these skills will bring.

○ Praise, praise and praise some more!

Measuring self-esteem in children

The importance of good self-esteem in children cannot be overestimated, especially as a lack of self-esteem has been shown to result in a downward spiral of multiple failure, the expectation of failure and also guilt and loss of confidence.

In 1967, as part of his seminal work into the contributing factors to self-esteem, US psychologist Stanley Coopersmith devised a questionnaire designed to measure a child's perception of her own confidence. He also further analyzed each child's relationship with his or her parents. His findings (published in his book *The Antecedents of Self-esteem*) were that high self-esteem in the 10- and 11-year-old boys who took part in the study was related directly to the following factors:

○ The high degree of acceptance, approval and affection shown by their parents.

○ The clearly defined limits laid down by the parents for the boys' behaviour.

More ways to nurture confidence

Having said all this, the single greatest way of building confidence in children is to show them our unconditional love – and this can't be stressed too greatly. This means continuing to express our love to them even on occasions when our children may not be our favourite people, and

O The fact that the parents took time and trouble to explain wrongdoing to their children, rather than just disciplining them with punishments or coercing them.

O The generous extent to which parents involved the children in making family decisions and showed how they valued their contributions.

Conversely, those boys with low self-esteem came from families where the parents showed little or no interest in them as individuals, and either ruled with a rod of iron or set no boundaries or framework for behaviour at all. Coopersmith deduced that these boys had developed a poor opinion of themselves as a result of feeling generally unappreciated by their parents.

From his research, Coopersmith concluded that allowing children a degree of freedom and autonomy within pre-set boundaries – and respecting them as individuals – resulted in higher self-esteem in children. His seminal work continues to be supported by research.

saying things like: 'I don't like what you're doing just now, but I will always love you'. It's another of those skills that doesn't always come easily – especially because it's quite natural to assume that our children know how much we love them and that this will never change. Natural, yes – but wrong. Just as your relationship with your partner needs to

be worked at, your relationship with your children needs to be fed, nourished and nurtured in equal measure, if not more so.

Besides this, there are a few general principles of behaviour that can help children and adults alike to feel more confident. One is that children who are conditioned to expect certain responses in given situations will feel confident they can predict outcomes; equally they may become insecure if the goalposts are moving constantly.

If, for example, you are consistent about bedtimes during the school week but are usually more flexible at weekends, your child will feel comfortable with asking for the privilege of staying up late on a Friday or a Saturday to watch a particular programme, or starting a game after dinner which has a lengthy playing time, confident that she is still within generally accepted boundaries. If, however, you suddenly alter the rules and insist on your child going to bed at her regular time on a weekend night without giving a specific reason for the change, her confidence may be lost: if rules can change like this, the security of consistency appears to be under threat in all areas.

For this reason, try to avoid making sudden rule changes without warning or offering a valid reason. If, for instance, you feel exhausted and so you try to bring your child's bedtime forward by an hour in order that you can have an evening to yourself as well as an early night, this will probably be met with resentment and confusion. Offering an explanation (and advance warning, if possible) when rule changes are about to occur is less likely to cause disruption and rebellion: telling a reluctant child that bedtime will be early tonight because you are all getting up for an early start in the morning, for example, is a lot more understandable than simply saying 'because I want you in bed now'.

Building on your child's strengths is a great way of empowering her. Whether she's good at playing a musical instrument; winning at top trumps; making up funny stories or getting herself dressed, encourage her to practise these skills often – and if she enjoys an audience, make time whenever you can to watch her and praise her efforts.

Each time your child feels a sense of achievement, her confidence will grow.

It's a good idea to let her do something she's particularly good at immediately before introducing a new skill or trying something she's less confident about: this way she should still be on a high from having succeeded, so she will feel more inclined to stretch herself in other directions and try new challenges. If she doesn't manage the new skill so well and is feeling a little down on herself, give her the opportunity to demonstrate one of her better abilities afterwards. If your child finds it difficult to hold on to her confidence, maybe you could remind her of her successes or produce evidence that she has managed a difficult task well in the past. Does she have any dancing, swimming or other sporting certificates you could bring out, for instance? Or maybe

you have a video or photo of the first time she rode her bike successfully? This could be just the reminder she needs, at a time when she is not feeling at her confident best, that she can achieve great things.

Avoid openly criticizing or correcting your young child whenever you can. If, for example, she consistently uses poor grammar ('I wented upstairs by myself'), repeat what she has said, but in its correct form: 'You went upstairs by yourself, did you? Clever girl!'. Don't point out her mistake every time. Eventually she will adopt correct speech, whereas if you continually correct her, she may lose the inclination to make conversation at all.

Similarly, try not to criticize her choice of friends, because in doing so you'll be criticizing her judgement and thereby undermining her self-esteem. If you are very unhappy about the children that she's mixing with, there are ways of encouraging other friendships and reducing the emphasis on those you'd rather discourage.

The power of praise

Praise is a subject that I'll return to often throughout this book, because it's impossible to underestimate the power of praise when building a child's – or an adult's – confidence. Whatever the level, praise gives us a boost that nothing else can match. Of course, not every achievement warrants a standing ovation: sometimes a simple acknowledgement of effort is enough to instil a real sense of pride.

Indeed, by school age many children can detect insincerity, however well meant, and will appreciate praise in proportion to achievement more readily than a lot of over-the-top cheering and rapturous applause.

So what is most important is that we make a point of rewarding effort in our children, however small it is. When your baby accepts a taste of an unfamiliar food; when she hugs you back; when she stops pulling your hair after you have asked her to: praise her. Even if she doesn't have any vocabulary yet, she will understand you inference simply by the tone of your voice. With school-age children and older, praise is far more effective when it's specific: so when your child carries her empty plate from the table to the kitchen, instead of simply saying 'Good girl', say: 'Good girl. Taking your own plate out is really helpful'. When she says 'please' after asking you for a drink, say: 'It's great to hear you asking me nicely' and when she gets into bed as soon as you ask her, say: 'Thanks for getting in quickly. It gives us more time for a story'.

Your pre-teen will be mortified if you go over the top with praise – especially in front of her friends ('Mu-um! You're embarrassing me!') – but it's still important to acknowledge her special efforts. When she asks to use the phone, thank her for asking; when she wears a smart outfit for a family event, thank her and tell her you appreciate it wouldn't have been her first choice; when she settles to her homework without a fuss, tell her how impressed you are with her behaviour.

It's better to praise what your child does, rather than what she is. If you say, for example: 'You are so patient' after she has shown great tolerance with a younger sibling, she may actually feel undeserving of this accolade because she knows that at other times she has been anything but patient. If, however, you say: 'You have been so patient this afternoon playing with your brother', she is more likely to feel satisfied with herself for having managed to behave nicely on this occasion. She's also more likely to try to be patient again next time if she doesn't feel she has to live up to a permanent label! The use of emotional language to highlight what your child has done also gives her an extra seal of approval, so say: 'I love it when you share' or 'It makes me really happy when you use kind words', and let her really see your pleasure.

From time to time you'll want to surprise your child with a small gift by way of a reward and, of course, this can be pleasing all round (these little tokens may even become treasured possessions), but a few well-chosen, specific words can be equally precious. I still remember my dad announcing to the family one Sunday morning (I would have been nine or ten at the time): 'You can always tell when Hilary's cooked breakfast because it looks hotel standard', and I recall the bristling pride I felt. I'm sure this is partly why I have always been a confident cook. I don't suppose Dad would have been able to recall, even a day later, what it was he'd said that had had such a great impact, but that's the power of praise – and long may it last!

How praise is received by your child

Praise is such a validating and bolstering commodity, and yet it's not something that we mete out or accept readily – which is all the more reason why we must make conscious efforts to praise our children.

If your child can accept praise willingly, knowing that it is meant sincerely, you will be doing a great job. Too many children are so taken aback by praise (usually because they are unaccustomed to receiving it) that they find it hard to accept and awkward to acknowledge. Teaching self-praise means showing your child how to notice her own achievements and give herself a pat on the back. This leads to a level of self-awareness that can help children feel great about themselves.

How boys and girls differ in social development

Only a couple of decades ago, boys were considered to be the 'stronger sex' – better at physically demanding tasks, academia and assertiveness. However, boys are increasingly being challenged by girls and now have to find a new kind of identity. As girls outstrip boys in academic achievement, compete with the best of them in physical pursuits and demand to be heard as an equal voice, to-day's boys are being forced to find a new definition for

'masculinity' and to carve a new role for themselves in modern society.

There are some things about boys that are intrinsic, though, regardless of their changing position in society. Firstly, studies have proven that boys do appear to find it harder to articulate their feelings than girls. This can mean that they struggle with ambivalent or negative feelings, and it can also mean that they find it harder to ask for help when they really need it – either socially or in school. Secondly, many boys have a surfeit of energy that needs to find an outlet each day (just as an exuberant puppy benefits enormously from plenty of regular exercise, so do most young boys), and yet our culture today is based on far more sedentary pursuits, such as surfing the internet, playing computer games and watching TV.

Girls, on the other hand, have a different set of issues that need to be recognized. Because girls have, historically, been expected to 'conform' to gender stereotypes (more so than boys) many feel the pressure to learn the roles of nurturer, housekeeper and caregiver, whilst at the same time trying to achieve both in and out of school – and attempting to make a strike for independence. But setting such high expectations can present a serious threat to their self-confidence if girls feel that they are failing in any of these areas.

As parents, then, we can take positive steps to help our different-sex children to develop socially. For boys this means providing positive male role models and regular opportunities for physical play in their daily lives, as well as coaching them in how to express themselves effectively and assertively, without resorting to aggression. For girls it means allowing our daughters to see our own inadequacies and to witness our failures so that they feel comfortable if they themselves fall short. Try to take the pressure off them with regard not only to continuous achievement, but also to homemaking skills. Of course it's great to show them the way in these areas (and boys, too), but we must also cut them plenty of slack so they realize they don't have to be brilliant at everything.

What children say about confidence

'My dad taught me to play cricket from when I was really little – I don't even remember starting now, but I know I was about two years old. Now I'm captain of the Year 7 cricket team, which feels brilliant. It was great to start a new school and feel good at something straight away, and it helped me make loads of new friends because the boys who wanted to be picked for the team were being really nice to me. I'm not all that good at maths and English and stuff, so I was a bit worried about feeling stupid in high school, but everyone knows me as the cricket captain, which means more to me anyway!'

STUART, 11, FROM CO. DURHAM

'I can really remember my first day in the infants' school. I didn't go to the school nursery so I didn't know anyone and I was really shy of talking to other children. I think I cried quite a lot at first, but the teachers were really kind to me. Then my teacher asked if anyone knew a poem off by heart, and my mum had taught me to say Christopher Robin's poem 'Halfway Down' [by A. A. Milne] so I said it to the class. I just concentrated really hard and pretended I was saying it with Mummy, and I got a big clap at the end, which made me feel loads better. After, a girl called Martha (who's my best friend now) asked me to teach her the poem 'cause she really liked it.'

AMY, 7, FROM PETERBOROUGH

'My parents always compare me to other children: if I say I got eight out of ten in my spelling test, for instance, they will ask me straight away who got ten. Now I wish I'd never told them that we have these tests, because even if I think I've done well, it's never good enough, and that makes me feel bad. Sometimes I wonder if they'd be happy if I got ten out of ten every week, or whether they'd just find something else to criticize. I can't wait to finish school for good, and I don't want to go to university if I'm going to be under this sort of pressure. The trouble is, if I tell them how I feel I'll probably just get told off.'

TROY, 11, FROM CARDIFF

'I like doing stuff with Mummy because she doesn't mind if I get it wrong. My best things are making sweets for people, playing cards and learning songs. Mummy and I both laugh if I get something wrong, and sometimes Mummy gets it wrong too so then we laugh at her. It's fun doing new stuff. It doesn't matter if you're no good because if you practise you get better and better. If I don't like something we just don't do it any more.'

ALICIA, 6, FROM GUILDFORD

'The first time I tried to ride my bike I kept falling off and I didn't really want to get back on. Then my dad said that if I got good enough he'd take me to my favourite seaside place and we could ride along the seafront together. That made me want to keep practising, and a couple of days later I could stay on, turn a corner and brake by myself. We went to the seaside and had a really great time. Now I know that if I keep trying when something's hard, I can do it in the end. My dad's great at showing me how to do stuff.'

HARVEY, 8, FROM HAYWARDS HEATH

Learning to be a great friend

Children these days are socialized far more than any previous generation; right from babyhood they are integrated with other children in mother-and-baby groups, toddler clubs, pre-schools and nurseries. Once they reach school age, they are thrust into classes of up to 30 children – sometimes more – and are frequently involved in after-school activities with children of the same age. All of this means that now, more than ever, it's vital that we teach our children the social skills that will enable them to accept and be accepted within peer groups.

Of course, not all babies and children can be nurtured into outgoing, gregarious individuals – some allowance has to be made for different personality types. However, with positive input from early on, even shy or reticent children can be equipped to feel self-assured and confident in social settings.

Give your baby a head start

Babies are hard-wired to be sociable, and this has been proven by many research studies. Experiments carried out as early as nine minutes after birth have suggested, for example, that babies prefer to look at faces rather than other objects; other studies have shown that babbling babies seem to understand one another.

So, given that newborns are ready and eager to face their world – and, more especially, the people in it – what can we do to help them develop social skills? There is quite a number of things, some of which may seem inappropriate to the age of a newborn or young baby, but which nonetheless can help 'condition' babies before they are ready to utilize their new skills.

Action plan

Help your baby become more sociable

o Once your baby seems to be settled (insofar as he is used to his daily routine and seems ready for new experiences), introduce him to different people in various social settings: take him to the park in his pram; put him in a sling and go to the local shop or join a mother-and-baby group where he will come across other babies and children. Let your baby set the pace to a degree, though, as overwhelming him with new contacts might just backfire and make him clingy. Don't expect him to display much sociability when he enters the 'separation anxiety' phase, either; this occurs in many babies from around seven months.

o Another research study has shown that by about six months of age a baby can distinguish his own name from other words in a sentence, and he most easily learns the meaning of the word or words which follow his name. Knowing this can help you to give your baby a head start with vocabulary by saying: 'Is that Tom's teddy?' or 'Let Mummy get Tom's spoon', and so on.

o Learning baby sign language can empower your baby from way before he can actually speak, and could help to make him more sociable, especially if he enjoys using the

signs he learns. You can find out about local signing classes by enquiring at your library, or about signing in general by contacting Tiny Talk, a company which offers classes all over the UK. You can even become a teacher yourself and run your own classes (see Resources for website address).

◉ Even if you don't go along the route of baby signing, you can still teach your baby to wave 'hello' and 'bye-bye', which is a great first step to sociability. This will quickly teach him that he is pleasing other people, as they are likely to return his greeting with a smile and an encouraging tone of voice.

◉ Introduce your baby to the idea of interpreting body language by sitting in front of a mirror with him on your lap and playing games together, such as peek-a-boo, or making facial expressions. He'll soon pick up on what makes you happy, and himself, and his interaction with you will help prepare him for interacting with other children.

Preparing toddlers and older children for friendships

Being able to form friendships is all part of becoming a well-rounded person, and by encouraging appropriate skills you will give your child a head start, not only in making approaches to potential new friends, but in placing appropriate value on the relationships formed from these early alliances. We have discussed already confidence boosting in the previous chapter, so here are some other ways in which you can prepare your child for new friendships.

Talking about feelings

It can be really helpful to your child if you can demonstrate to him how highly you value the importance of friendships in your own life. Talk to your child about how much the friendships you made in early childhood still mean to you. Say, for example: 'Friends who have known me for most of my life are great to share memories with – and they're the ones who understand me best of all.'

If you're not still in touch with friends from that far back, emphasize how much the friends you have now mean to you in adulthood, and draw comparisons between these feelings and those of your child. You could say, for instance: 'I really like having my best friend to chat to whenever I'm feeling a bit down; it's really important to me. Do you feel like that?' or 'I don't always want to burden Daddy with little worries, and sometimes it's really useful to have someone outside the family to talk things over with. Do you do that with your friends?' or 'Isn't it great to be able to invite different people over to spend time with us? It's a real blessing to have good friends'.

Sharing experiences

Talking about your own experiences of friendship can be a good opening gambit in getting your child to share his. Say, for example: 'I felt a bit scared when I first started school, but as soon as I made a few friends I didn't feel so worried any more. How did you feel before you made friends?' or 'I can remember the first person I ever thought

of as a real friend. Can you?'. You should be able to get a sense of whether or not your child is comfortable talking about these things, and if he isn't – or if he can't come up with answers to your questions – you may need to step in to help him forge friendships of his own (see page 76).

If you think your child may have suffered a few knock-backs when trying to start friendships, you can share your own experiences (or make some up!). Try saying: 'It can be really hard sometimes to make friends, isn't it? I remember wanting to be part of a group of children and no one letting me in. Has that happened to you?'. Then discuss between you strategies for overcoming the problem. Maybe you could ask one or two of the children to tea together so that your child doesn't have the awkwardness of a one-to-one. Or you could arrange to meet some of the school mums and their children in the park one afternoon. (For more advice on overcoming confidence knocks, see Chapter 5.)

Recognizing non-verbal cues

There are many non-verbal messages flying around in any social circle, including raised eyebrows, general posture, facial expressions and personal proximity or distance. Some of these signs will be too subtle for your child to understand (especially when he is pre-school age), but even at this stage there are some you can teach him to be aware of.

Use role play to experiment with how different postures and non-verbal cues can make him feel: try folding your

arms and frowning; shrugging your shoulders and looking away; smiling and leaning forward, and so on. Switch
roles and describe how you are feeling when he makes certain gestures. It could be that your child is misinterpreting
other children's non-verbal signals, thereby missing out on
opportunities to make friends. If, for instance, another child
purposefully edges towards your child during a mum-and-
toddler group play session, but doesn't make eye contact,
this could still mean that that child feels comfortable with
yours and would like to play alongside him. (In any case,
at the toddler stage, children tend to play alongside rather
than actively with each other.) In some situations it may be
that you'll need to help your child to make the next move
to strike up a friendship, if you think he would like to (see
page 76).

Of course, an older child may be more clued up on body
language and other non-verbal cues than you are! Your
child might be able to read these signs without actually
being aware of them, in which case by making him aware
you may help him to interpret signals more accurately. Talk
to him about which gestures and postures feel more open
and friendly to him, and which he thinks are more likely to
send out the message 'Leave me alone!'.

Understanding humour

Most children appreciate humour to varying degrees,
although many will remain oblivious to all but the most
obvious kinds until they are well into their primary school

years. Even at this stage, whether they 'get' certain types of humour or not depends on your own use of it. If you as parents tend to use sarcastic humour, or if you like to poke fun at each other, your child is likely to pick up on this and may even start doing it himself. In this case he will understand it when he experiences it himself from other sources, but beware: your child and others may misconstrue this humour and end up feeling ridiculed and isolated.

It's very helpful in all cases to try to teach your child to laugh at himself occasionally. Obviously, no one enjoys being the constant butt of the joke, but learning not to take ourselves too seriously is one way of breaking the ice and getting along with other people.

Sharing and turn-taking

As we have seen in Chapter 1, children up to around the age of three are primarily egocentric, with little regard for the feelings of others. They can also be particularly territorial. Of course, this is hardly surprising: very few things are truly theirs, and as a result they may be loath to share what they do have!

As well as sharing, turn-taking is an acquired skill, and one that tends to come when children are required to queue and wait at school (or earlier, in places such as at nursery). The best grounding you can give any child in sharing and turn-taking is to practise it at home and with friends. Start when your child is still a baby by sharing food with him. Once he is able to accept some solids, share a banana, an apple or some other food. Cut up the fruit and put it on your plate, then pass him pieces so he really feels he's sharing your meal with you. Let him see you sharing with other friends and family members: offer food around the table; have a sip of your partner's tea. When he is used to sharing your food, encourage him to share his, too: cut the last piece of cake in half and share it between your child and his friend.

Another way you can encourage sharing is by buying only one toy or game to be shared between your child and his friends or siblings – a tactic which will also encourage turn-taking. A young child can find it hard to wait for his turn, so make it easier for him by having something on hand to absorb him while he waits; or you could reward his patience with a cuddle, a few words of praise or the promise of a trip to the park (as long as it will happen on the same day!). With your older child, play board games regularly as a family; encourage each player to be aware of the other players' progress and to take an interest in the general progress of the game (rather than just his own position within it), and keep to the rules of taking turns.

When teaching your child to share and take turns, do try to see things from his point of view, too. Before friends come round, let him hide away one or two of his treasured toys and games, and don't insist that these are shared; similarly, don't always make him put everyone else before himself – he is every bit as entitled to go first as the next child, as long as he appreciates that everyone else must

have the same opportunity. By doing this you are letting your child see that it's quite fair for him to keep some of his own personal possessions as his very own, and that it's okay for him to put himself first in various situations, but that what matters most is that everyone is given equal consideration – regardless of their age or position in the family – and that the same applies to friends and relatives, too.

Learning respect

The ability to show respect is one that stands children in good stead when it comes to building successful relationships in both childhood and adulthood. Explaining the concept of respect to a child is best done simply. You could say, for example, that respecting people is about considering their feelings as much as our own; treating them as we would like to be treated ourselves; sometimes putting them first; listening to their point of view (even if we don't agree with it every time) and showing them how to behave with politeness and courtesy.

This is another lesson that is best taught by your own example – this means showing respect to your children as well as to other adults. It's easy to confuse showing respect to children with being too soft, but the two things are quite separate: it's perfectly possible to show respect within the normal framework of house rules and discipline.

So, starting today, make a conscious effort to show more respect to your child by, for example, encouraging him to express his opinions without interruption or contradiction;

letting him have his own way sometimes (but not always, as this gives mixed messages about whether or not you are worthy of his respect!); making an effort to appreciate the things that he likes, trying to understand why he's turned off by or is fearful of others; and by remembering to say 'please' and 'thank you' to him. (These are courtesies often reserved for our adult peers, but which are equally important when interacting with children.)

Give and take

It's easy for children – especially pre-schoolers – to regard as friends only those people who are unconditionally kind to them, and this is why so many immature associations founder and fail to thrive. A key point for your child to understand and appreciate is that all successful relationships are built on a two-way process of give and take. Yes, of course it feels wonderful to be praised, cuddled, appreciated and given little gifts by people around us – after all, we all need a degree of love, respect and approval in order to feel like worthwhile human beings; but therein lies the point: just as we need these psychological and emotional 'strokes', so do those people doing the stroking. So if your child dismisses a playmate because 'he's not being kind to me any more', once you have established the reasons behind this change of attitude you can gently remind your child that the responsibility for keeping the friendship going is his as well as his friend's, and that kindness must be given as well as received.

Reinforce this idea by letting your child see your happiness whenever he shows you consideration. Most young children are eager to please their parents (at least until they reach school age!) so you can seize this period as a time to capitalize on his innate benevolence. Next time your child gives you one of his soft toys to cuddle or offers you one of his sweets without being asked to, show your pleasure with a big smile, a hug and a kiss. In these ways, your child will see that kindness brings its own rewards, and that to give can be just as pleasurable as to receive.

Showing appreciation

An important quality (touched on in the previous section) that popular children and adults tend to share is the ability to show appreciation – and it's a skill that many adults, as well as children, could do well to learn! How often, for instance, have you taken your partner for granted? Do you make a point of saying 'please' and 'thank you', or have you let such courtesies slide because it's 'only them'? Does your partner always acknowledge and appreciate the little things that you do for him? When he does, how does that make you feel? And what about when he doesn't?

It costs nothing to express appreciation, and yet the rewards can be rich indeed – especially for the person who is on the receiving end. The same applies to childhood friendships; teach your child to say kind things to others and – as long as he is being sincere – his popularity should grow! My own eight-year-old daughter, Natasha, was paid a special compliment by a schoolfriend recently, who told her that she has a special quality that makes everything she takes part in fun. When she was relating this to us, Natasha made the rather touching comment: 'That's something I can lock in my heart for ever'. Those few kind words meant more to her than a shared packet of sweets ever could.

Listening and empathizing

These are qualities that are easier to nurture in school-age children than pre-schoolers, but the earlier you can try to reinforce them, the better. As with sharing, the best way to do this is to lead by example.

Start by showing your child that effective listening includes staying quiet until the other person has finished what they are saying, then repeating the message back to show you have understood. You can do this over and over again with your child, partner and friends – and your child will hopefully pick up on it and do it eventually himself, too. Here's an example:

YOUR CHILD: *'Sometimes I think no one wants to be my friend because I get left on my own in the playground and then I get lonely and sad.'*

YOU: *'So being left without anyone to play with makes you feel sad, and you wish other children would include you in the playground?'*

Empathizing is one step on from simply listening and requires you to put yourself in another's situation and to try to really experience the feelings that the other

person may be feeling. To help your child to understand how he can do this, you could demonstrate your own empathy in a continuation of the first scenario:

YOU: *'That must feel very upsetting and I expect it makes you wonder why other children aren't playing with you. I can understand how that makes you feel sad; I think I'd be sad, too.'*

Another effective way of teaching listening skills and empathy from a young age is to read books or watch DVDs together where the story has a moral theme. A story like *Cinderella*, for instance, where the main character suffers not only the loss of her mother, but the meanness of her stepfamily and the lack of support from her father, but who ultimately wins the hand of the charming prince and lives happily ever after, is a perfect vehicle for introducing the skills of listening and empathy.

Start by asking your child which bits of the story really stuck in his mind, then help him to explore how Cinderella must have felt. Ask questions such as: 'What do you think it would feel like to be forced to do all the housework and never to be given any treats?'; 'What sort of people do you think Cinderella's stepsisters are?'; 'How do you think Cinderella felt when the sisters were getting ready to go to the ball without her?'; 'Why do you think the prince loved Cinderella and not her stepsisters?' and 'Why do you think Cinderella deserved to be the happiest of all in the end?'.

With an older child, play games where he has to think about feelings – for example, ask him to list all the words he can that are similar in meaning to 'happy' or 'sad'. Ask him to pull happy, sad, cross, excited and frightened faces. Make up stories together where you can both act out the emotions described above. Get your child to come up with as many ways as he can in which other children and adults make him happy (but try to avoid material things, such as being bought lavish gifts!). For example, by listening to his ideas; by appreciating his schoolwork; by inviting him to parties; by including him on their teams; by paying him compliments, and so on.

Unacceptable behaviour

Some children – and this is particularly true of pre-schoolers, although it can also be the case amongst some older children – are unaware that some of their behaviour might be regarded by others as antisocial (not in an ASBO sense, but from the point of view of manners and courtesy!). Pushing, jostling, snatching and refusing to share create barriers for children of all ages when they are trying to make friends – and these behaviours won't go down well with playleaders or teachers, either.

Biting, hitting, hair-pulling, spitting and swearing are completely unacceptable in any social setting and should, of course, be discouraged at all times, regardless of the situation. If your young child displays any of these traits, one way of teaching him that his behaviour is unacceptable is to show your disapproval by withdrawing your attention. First, remove him firmly from the situation, whilst

quietly explaining what he has done wrong; then transfer your attention to the child at the receiving end of the behaviour, comforting and apologizing to him or her. When your child is calm, ask him to offer an apology, too. Conversely, if your child is at the receiving end of unacceptable behaviour at the hands of another child, comfort him and check he's okay before discussing together what was wrong with the other child's behaviour and why it was unacceptable.

In a playgroup or another play setting, observe the children who are playing nicely together and discuss with your child what behaviours they are displaying that make them friends: sharing a toy; enjoying a joke; playing a game together; smiling at each other; taking turns – these are all the kinds of behaviour that will enable your child to make friends with other children.

Helping him make contact

A great many children – even those who appear to be confident and outgoing – find it very hard to approach an unknown child and make contact. This is perfectly under-standable; just like reticent adults, they are worried about how they will feel if they are rejected, and would probably rather the first approach happened the other way round!

An important way you can help your child to make new friends is to step in and make the first contact yourself. In this way, you'll be showing your child how he can start a conversation with others. Say, for example, you move to a new area and discover the local park. You could get talking

to other mums, ask their children's names and introduce
your child to them. Or you could encourage your child to
interact with another child: 'Why don't you show Liam your
new stickers?'. The worst that can happen is that your child
refuses – in which case you can say: 'Well, it seems he's
feeling a bit shy today; perhaps another time...' without
your child losing face.

Don't worry if you have no success initially – it's quite
normal to get no response on either side the first time you
try – but if you keep visiting the park you may see the same
faces again and again, and the more times that you make
contact the more comfortable your child is likely to feel.
You can use the same tactic at mother-and-toddler groups,
baby gym sessions, on holidays where you see the same
families repeatedly, and in many other social situations.

**There's nothing quite as uplifting as watching your child
striking up a friendship and playing contentedly alongside
another child who, just a few minutes ago, was a complete stranger. We adults could learn a lot from this very
open behaviour!**

If your child is very shy, do let his other carers know so that
they can also help to integrate him with other children. If
your child is in childcare, ask his nursery keyworker, childminder or nanny to facilitate some new contacts.

There are pros and cons in each childcare setting when
it comes to making new friends: in a nursery there will be

plenty of children for your child to mix and mingle with, so he's got more chances of finding some like-minded toddlers to play with, whereas at a childminder's the group of children will be smaller and probably of mixed ages. This can be an advantage if he prefers small groups or if he prefers to baby other children or be babied himself; on the other hand, it means he will have less scope for making friends if the other children under the minder's care don't appeal to him so much. With a nanny, the situation will be more or less the same as it would be if he was with you, in that you'll need to ask her to take him into social settings and make a few approaches on his behalf.

Action plan
How to practise social skills with your child

O Set up a reward scheme, such as a star chart, by which your child can earn stickers, points or pennies in return for good behaviour when he is with other children and adults. This behaviour should involve turn-taking, sharing, behaving politely and respectfully, and any other efforts made to be considerate to others.

O Go through his DVDs or videos and books and pick out those with storylines involving empathy. Make a point of watching or reading one or more a week, then discussing with your child the themes within it and their relevance to his life.

O Pinpoint some time each day when you can sit down without distractions and talk to your child, tailoring the level of conversation to his age and understanding. You may find him more responsive if you talk whilst he is engaged in a fun activity, such as cooking with you, eating his favourite meal or colouring in. Centre your chat around what makes him happy and unhappy – particularly about friendships. Bring your own experiences into the conversation so that your child learns that building successful relationships requires the same skills whether you're a child or an adult.

○ Use language in your day-to-day conversation that will reinforce the messages of turn-taking and sharing: 'Whose turn is it to clear the table?'; 'Come on, let's share the last biscuit'; 'It's your turn to pick a card' or 'Would you like some of my pudding?'.

○ Role-play some friendship games with your child, using his teddies and other cuddly toys as his friends. Perhaps Teddy could be feeling left out of things; or maybe your child's favourite cuddly toy has hurt himself. It's only a small leap for your child to make from comforting a toy to knowing how to comfort a friend.

○ Take it in turns with your child to guess each other's feelings from your body language. You could do this whilst sharing a meal or walking to school if you don't have time to make a game of it in its own right.

○ Consciously make an effort to laugh at yourself instead of getting angry and frustrated when things go wrong. This will encourage your child to do the same himself.

Friendship and the child with special needs

All children have the same need to be loved, nurtured and encouraged in all areas of development – regardless of whether their development is typical or not. In many cases, children with special needs who are able to be integrated into mainstream schools are treated as equals within the classroom and, usually, within the playground, too. It's very encouraging to find, especially amongst the younger age groups, that children today will often happily accept, support and befriend children who are in some way different to themselves in terms of physical, educational or emotional needs.

Nowadays, far more children with special needs are entering the mainstream school system and are thriving within it; many schools have a good network of learning support teachers and specially-trained classroom assistants. By law, children with physical or mental disabilities cannot be discriminated against, so there are many more opportunities for these children to feel that they are a part of normal life than ever before.

In recent years there has been plenty of research into the advantages for children with special needs of being integrated with able children – and there are many. Firstly, the earlier a child with special needs mixes and socializes with his peer group, the more likely he is to be accepted for who, not what, he is; so do take part in mother-and-baby groups and other social groups as early on as you can. If you are planning on using childcare and your child is able to attend a mainstream nursery or other pre-school provision, then do let him join in. Here he is likely to learn about routines, how to participate in everyday life, the importance of discipline and cooperation and how to adapt to a group of different people. This will help to equip him for life at school as well as outside it, and for everyday life in general. It will also enable him to appreciate that, although he may have more needs than his peers, he doesn't warrant special attention in all situations and that the needs of others are of equal importance.

Both your child and those he befriends will be able to learn a lot from each other – your child may, for example, find new ways of communicating with his peers and begin to appreciate the benefits of give and take in conversation, as well as the power of communication itself. He may also find ways to increase his dexterity, learn how things work, discover how to play effectively and how to get on with self care (where appropriate), but most of all he'll have lots of fun and will appreciate being accepted for himself.

His friends will also benefit from their relationship with him and will learn an important lesson in how to relate to and tolerate people whose behaviour or level of development is different from the norm, and not to build prejudices. As a result, they will start to appreciate that 'different' doesn't equal 'bad' and they will learn new skills for communicating with their less able friends, which can then translate into the rest of their social life.

Children who are integrated with peers who have special needs tend to grow up to be more accepting of people with disabilities than they would otherwise, which is a great prospect for the future of society.

The integrated experience is also beneficial for teachers and other childcare providers, who will develop a more accepting and positive attitude towards disabled people than they might otherwise. The special skills they will need to hone will also equip them for looking after children of all ability levels.

Some children with more severe disabilities do require the extra facilities, attention and focus of special schools, but the importance of friendships is as relevant to them as it is to mainstream children and, depending on the degree of disability, the relevant areas of advice within this book can still be applied. Talk to your child's school about any concerns you might have and you will discover that they will have particular strategies in place to nurture and encourage friendships.

Children on the qualities of a good friend

'A good friend is somebody that you can trust with your secrets.'

THOMAS, 8, MANCHESTER

'A friend listens to you without interrupting and is always there for you, no matter what.'

NINA, 10, CARSHALTON

'My best friend is someone I can share my favourite things with.'

ROBERT, 7, NEWCASTLE

'A real friend is someone who accepts you just as you are.'

REBECCA, 11, LINCOLN

'To make a friend, you have to like them.'

ELLIE, 6, DEVON

'A good friend is a person who helps you with problems.'

IOAN, 9, CARDIFF

'I like friends who are kind, comforting and funny!'

JOSHUA, 11, GREAT YARMOUTH

'Friends are the people you feel happiest around.'

SALLY-ANNE, 12, MANCHESTER

'Whenever you need them, they are there for you.'

LEANDRA, 9, TOWER HAMLETS

'A true friend is someone you feel totally comfortable with.'

SAYID, 10, NOTTINGHAM

'A good friend shouldn't talk about you behind your back or just go off you when someone else asks them to be friends.'

ALI, 11, KINGSTON-UPON-THAMES

Famous quotes on friendship

'Am I not destroying my enemies when I make friends of them?'

ABRAHAM LINCOLN

'A friend is someone who knows the song in your heart and can sing it back to you when you have forgotten the words.'

UNKNOWN

'A friend is a gift you give yourself.'

ROBERT LOUIS STEVENSON

'The only way to have a friend is to be one.'

RALPH WALDO EMERSON

'There are no such things as strangers, only friends we haven't met yet.'

ANONYMOUS

'You can hardly make a friend in a year, but you can easily offend one in an hour.'

CHINESE PROVERB

'If I had to choose between betraying my country and betraying my friend, I hope I should have the guts to betray my country.'

E. M. FORSTER   (WITH THANKS TO WWW.THEROMANTIC.COM)

Encouraging self-reliance

Friendships in early childhood do not always endure, and this is partly because some personality pairs, or groups, are more compatible than others, and partly because anyone who is willing to play or interact with your child at any given time may be regarded, however fleetingly, as a friend. This is particularly true of toddlers and pre-schoolers.

However, the longevity and value of these relationships does tend to increase with age as children mature and become aware of which personalities and character types bring out the best – and the worst – in them. The key to your child recognizing this difference is allowing her to build up her self-reliance so that she can accept herself as she is, then helping her to celebrate her individuality while also showing her how to do the same with other people.

What is self-reliance?

There's a subtle difference between being self-confident and being self-reliant. You may find that people are self-confident in specific areas of their lives: you may know someone, for instance, who regards himself as a proficient footballer; perhaps you have a friend who seems confident in her ability to communicate effectively with others; some of us may believe ourselves to be great parents. What sets self-reliant individuals apart, however, is their ability to trust their own judgement and to carve a path for themselves through life without needing always to consult with others or seek outside approval. It's a fantastic skill to have,

The self-reliant individual will feel able to cope with all that life throws at her with equanimity. Rather than fretting about problems, she will find ways of solving them; she has good control over her life.

and one that can increase personal happiness as well as attract the admiration and attention of other, less self-reliant people.

How to teach self-reliance

So can children be taught self-reliance? Surely they need us, as parents, to guide and advise them and to step in and do things for them? Well, yes, to an extent – but as our children grow and develop we can afford to delegate certain responsibilities and, little by little, let them begin to take the reins of their own lives. In fact, your child's self-reliance will come from being given opportunities to think, feel and act for herself.

Whilst we don't want to burden our children with too much responsibility before they're ready, it's all too easy to continue doing things for them that we have always done, without noticing that they are either dexterous enough, have the appropriate skills or are sufficiently confident to have a go themselves! I'm as guilty of this as anyone: for example, I continued to take on the task of cleaning out Poppy the hamster's cage long after my daughter, Natasha, was able to do it unsupervised: I had simply forgotten to reassess Natasha's ability. It was only on a day when I had

101 things to do and couldn't fit Poppy into the equation that I decided to take a chance and see whether Natasha might manage the job well enough by herself. I needn't have worried – if anything she made a better job of it than I could, and she's been doing it herself ever since (although, at age eight, she does still need reminding!).

The point is that children need to be allowed to motivate themselves and to trust their own judgement in order to become independent – and, as long as they know that help is always available if they should need it, most will relish the opportunity to be a bit more 'grown up'. Part of my blindness to Natasha's increasing competence was, I suspect, due to a subconscious desire to keep her young and dependent for as long as possible, but our children won't develop self-reliance if we cluck around them like mother hens. It's up to us to recognize their readiness and loosen the apron strings a bit at a time; leave it too late and you may have a true 'Mummy's girl/boy' on your hands. Add to this the thought that if we do everything for our children they are more likely to become lazy for life, and it's easier to feel the motivation.

The art of self-acceptance

In order for your child to learn to trust her instincts, she needs first to be able to accept herself just as she is – and the same is true of adults. Self-acceptance is, in turn, key to building good friendships. For many of us our natural inclination is to try to fit in with others – sometimes even at the expense of our own personalities, morals or integrity – which ultimately can be destructive and can leave adults and children alike feeling worthless when relationships fail. Whether your child is naturally reticent, outgoing, a little eccentric or more conventional, her sense of self needs to be nurtured – not only so she can boost her own confidence, but also in order for her to appreciate and value the individuality of others.

As long as she accepts who she is and is happy with herself, she will make friendships that validate her personality.

Nurturing your child's personality requires a subtle balance between responding to her on her own terms and building up those aspects which may otherwise cause her discomfort later on. For example, if your child is quiet, reflective and a little shy, taking an ebullient 'shake yourself out of it' approach could be very damaging to her self-esteem and her trust in you – a bit like trying a little rough-and-tumble with a nervous new puppy.

Of course, it's far more appropriate in such a case to take a more gentle, relaxed approach, but if your child has problems with, say, laughing at herself occasionally, a little coaching in the art of self-deprecation won't go amiss. The best way to go about this is to poke a little fun at yourself sometimes, perhaps when you have made a bit of a

hash of something – and even better is if you can make a favourable comparison with your child at the same time: 'Look at old butter-fingers here! Fully grown and I can't even keep hold of a bowl long enough to bring it to the table! I bet you'd have managed without dropping it'.

The ability to laugh at ourselves can also be born out of taking risks – and risk-taking is, in itself, a facet of self-reliance. Say, for example, your child accepts an invitation to a skating party without ever having skated before. She is very likely to fall over repeatedly before she finds her feet, and she must accept that she might not stay upright at all during that first experience of skating. If she is able to laugh at herself – which is part of accepting herself and her own limitations – she will get a lot out of the experience, will in all likelihood want to try again on another occasion and will probably win the admiration of her friends. At the same time, her friends will feel comfortable in her company because they will know that they are not going to get laughed at by her. If, on the other hand, she becomes upset or angry at her own failure, she will leave the party feeling undermined, upset and having left her friends with the impression that she is not such a good sport and would probably not be supportive of their own failures.

Whenever you can, get the message across to your child that the art of laughing at yourself can ultimately win you friends.

Power struggles in friendships

Many friendship pairings in childhood are based on a tacit understanding that one personality is stronger and therefore more influential than the other – meaning that the less out-going children may be forced to compromise themselves in order to feel valued. The attraction of opposite personality types is age-old and understandable: some people see in others qualities they feel they lack themselves, and so they enjoy these qualities vicariously. This can be healthy when each friend keeps his or her own set of values intact, but the fear of rejection – by one child or a group – drives some children into behaviours they know are wrong or that they feel uncomfortable with (see page 116). However, this can be avoided if you can build up your child's sense of self.

In this situation, as in others, our example as parents is crucial. How we behave in relation to our partners, peers, extended family and authority figures will influence the way in which our children relate to people around them. If, for instance, one partner in a relationship is domineering and fails to consider the feelings of the other, this sends the message that the needs of the dominant one are more im-portant and that the person who is not being considered is somehow less valued. When we argue, we should do all we can to reach a resolution by stepping down, cooling off, apologizing or forgiving. We need to demonstrate to our children that each individual is equally valuable and that, in any family, democracy should be the order of the day.

In practice, this means that our children should also be allowed a voice. Obviously, parents need to set limits, but it's not hard to allow children a little autonomy, independence and say in family decisions, where appropriate.

As for friendships, the important thing to impress upon our children is that they have as much right to an opinion and a say in what they do as anyone else. It may be that they are comfortable with an imbalance of 'power', and as long as they are genuinely happy and confident, we should leave well alone.

How to set boundaries – for your child and yourself!

You can empower your child to begin to trust her own judgement and become more self-reliant in lots of ways, but you should always remain clear about how broadly she can take control. In other words, spell out to her in which areas you will keep control and which are open to negotiation. As long as you're clear, your child will feel confident about beginning to make some choices and decisions of her own.

Encourage your child to spend time in free play; not only will this allow her time to think for herself, it will also give the self-motivation to decide how to fill her spare time. If she wants to try something new, resist the temptation to hover ready to rescue her if she runs into difficulties, and don't chip in with suggestions for the 'right' way to do things; she'll learn soon enough through trial and error. Similarly, don't rush to her aid every time she comes across a problem. Part of nurturing self-reliance means allowing children the time and space to work things out for themselves. They can easily become frustrated and give up if you are too quick to intervene, so wait for your child to ask you for help, rather than volunteering it up front.

Action plan
How to boost your child's sense of self-reliance

○ Consult her on small family matters – whether it is about going to the park or out for a bike ride over the weekend, for example.

○ Ask her opinion on things: for example, 'Does the vase of flowers look better here or over there?'

○ Display her artwork, homemade cards, cardboard models – or anything she has created and feels proud of.

○ Let her have a role in caring for younger siblings or family pets.

○ Give her opportunities to do 'grown-up' things that are appropriate to her age, such as helping to dry unbreakables; letting her have her own duster to help with the housework or showing her how to make herself a sandwich.

○ Allow her a degree of autonomy, depending on her age. Let her pick out her own clothes (with a younger child, it's best to offer a choice of several appropriate outfits you've selected beforehand, unless you don't mind her donning a

swimsuit and slippers or some other inappropriate get-up!); tell her you are trusting her to get her homework done without prompting; put her to bed 15 minutes early and let her read for a while before switching off her own light (if this appeals to her) or let her arrange her room how she likes it, even if it wouldn't be the way you'd have done it.

○ Shower your child with praise – don't make it dependent on her success, but give her due credit for the effort she puts in. Praise her, too, if she undertakes a task off her own bat – making her bed or getting dressed before being asked to do so, for example. Remember to use emotional language such as: 'I'm really proud of you' or 'I love it when you surprise me like that'. This will demonstrate to her the positive impact of her actions.

○ Resist belittling your child, however surprised you may be that she isn't able to undertake a task. You may have the urge to say: 'But most ten-year-olds would be able to do that *easily'*, but fight it! Instead, say: 'It's okay if you can't manage yet; let's leave it a little while longer and try again'.

Reinforcing right and wrong

If there is an unpleasant or undermining power struggle going on in one or more or your child's friendships – and you're fortunate enough to find out about it – you'll be able to intervene to an extent. This may mean taking a direct approach and broaching the subject with the other child or his parents (see page 120), or simply bolstering your child's sense of right and wrong and finding strategies for overcoming the more dominant child's influence.

With a younger child, clever ways of reinforcing right and wrong include role-playing with dolls and teddies, where you can initiate the scenario and encourage your child to play it out; watching favourite DVDs which contain a moral message and discussing the feelings of the characters involved; giving small rewards for good behaviour (not necessarily tangible – perhaps a star chart which promises a treat on completion); discussing which children your child likes most in her social group and why and pointing out good moral choices as your child – or other people around her – make them.

Encourage openness generally within your home, so that your child is unfamiliar with secrecy and subterfuge.

With an older child, moralizing will most likely fall on deaf ears, but initiating conversations at a more adult level and making yourself open to any discussion may produce better results. This will mean that you need to keep an open mind and an approachable attitude (which can be very challenging with pre-teens), but it will pay dividends if it means your child trusts you enough to confide in you. Try to accept whatever you are told without judgement or criticism, even if you are hearing something you would rather not. Often a reasoned discussion can take place only if you can create a calm atmosphere, not one laden with annoyance and outrage. Remember, pre-teens and teenagers will sometimes say things that are deliberately provocative and designed to test your reaction!

Again, one of the best ways to reinforce right and wrong is to lead by example, so give voice to some of your own internal struggles to show your child that, at times, you too have battles with yourself over doing the right thing, but that you do eventually come to a good decision. You could say, for example: 'I know Grandma would love to come to lunch again this weekend, but I was really hoping not to have to do any entertaining. I could invite her round for

Keep cool, but not too cool...

A word to the wise: usually it is considered deeply *un*cool amongst children of all ages when adults try to be cool, so avoid using pop culture references during the course of your discussions. Asking your child: 'What would Lizzie McGuire do?', for example, could not only make your child feel uncomfortable because you have intruded into her fantasy world, but could actually distract you both if your child starts recounting funny bits of dialogue from her favourite episode. Instead, get your child's own ideas on situations: 'How do you think that would make you feel?' or 'What do you think [your friend] could do to make things better?'. This will empower your child at the same time as saving you both from potential embarrassment.

afternoon tea instead of Sunday lunch – that would be a compromise. Yes, I'll give her a ring now'.

Celebrating individuality

The ability to trust one's own judgement, which is part of self-reliance, shows real strength of character, and children with a strong sense of self-reliance are often safer than those who lack it when placed in situations where they are vulnerable to unfavourable influences. It also puts them in the position whereby they are able to guide more vulnerable children towards making the right choices.

In order to build a sense of real conviction in our children, we must encourage and praise them as often as possible whenever they see a project through to the end. They may have some crazy-sounding plans, but as long as the objectives are not harmful, we should celebrate their imaginations and creativity, and applaud them when they carry things off.

Some children are positively eccentric, and this, too, should be celebrated and nurtured, as it shows a great sense of individuality. If we avoid making fun of our children's quirks, but instead show admiration for their sense of self, you will see their confidence in themselves grow.

Setting up scenarios to role-play with your child where you try to persuade her to do something against her judgement or wishes, is another effective way of training her to stand her ground and just be herself. Pretend, for example,

that her close friends have decided, quite spontaneously, that a particular fashion style is no longer cool, but it has just become your own child's favourite. Use this scenario to discuss with her why it would be stronger to stick with her first choice than to change her mind just to fit in. Discuss the difference between falling in with people to gain their approval, reaching a compromise that everyone can live with, or simply standing firm and having the courage of her convictions. Talk about situations where each of these decisions might be most appropriate. Next, you can move on to more serious role plays; perhaps something like saying no to drugs, if you feel it's appropriate. In this context you can reinforce the long-term advantages to steering clear of drugs, or other harmful substances, and talk about how the short-term appeal is not really positive at all.

Playing to your child's strengths

One excellent way of reinforcing and endorsing a child's individuality is to play to her strengths. If, for example, she is a great dancer or music enthusiast, see whether she might enjoy enrolling in dance classes or learning a musical instrument. If she is interested in words, encourage her to make up stories, or devise your own word games together. If sport is her thing, see if there is a local club she could join – or be brave and start your own team with the help of other local parents.

Key to this is recognizing what your child is good at. We can get so caught up in the everyday responsibilities of parenting – particularly in households where both parents work – that there is little time left to try new pursuits or just to notice where children's natural inclinations lie. It might help if you could build a regular slot into your weekly schedule where you try a different activity – it needn't be expensive or time-consuming: a game of tiddlywinks or hangman, for instance, takes minutes but could illustrate how accurate your child's aim is or how interested she is in spelling.

Don't limit each activity to only one attempt, either. The first time you try something, you may just have hit on a day when she isn't at her best or is coming down with something, so give each pursuit a fair crack of the whip.

Recognizing weak areas

By the same token, when you notice a weak area it may help your child to practise it and build up her skills – but this depends on how important it is likely to be in her social circle and how much she is bothered by her lack of ability. If, for example, her friends all enjoy playing skipping games, but she can't use a skipping rope so she feels left out, you could help her to get the hang of it by spending a little time practising with her. Perhaps she would get on better with a shorter rope? Or maybe she'd prefer one with tinsel tassels on the handles or the type that converts into a jump stick. If, on the other hand, a weak area is not going to be an issue amongst her wider social group and she is reluctant to practise, that's fine, too.

If your child is adamant that a particular pursuit is not for her, applying pressure, however gentle, could undermine her sense of self, rather than encourage it. If you find her attitude disappointing – because, for instance, you come from a musical family and she is reluctant to learn an instrument – it's equally important to back off. Remember, she's developing her own ideas and interests and whilst it certainly doesn't mean that she won't come back to this particular pursuit with renewed enthusiasm later on, what matters is that it will have been through her own choice. Meanwhile, continue to practise your own musical instrument around her so that she can see how much you enjoy it and how fulfilling it can be.

How to encourage decision-making

You can help your child to develop great judgement and to make wise decisions in several different ways. If you talk to her about the options available, she'll begin to learn how to reason things through; by sharing your own thought processes when you make decisions she'll discover what she needs to take into account and what she should disregard.

It's okay, too, for your child to make the occasional wrong decision – as long as it doesn't have catastrophic consequences. We all learn some of our most valuable lessons from our mistakes, and as long as we are supportive of our children ('Well, it didn't work out, but at least you tried') rather than critical ('I told you that would never work!'), these lessons can be very constructive. So if your child does make a mistake, spend some time talking to her about other ways in which she might have handled things and how the outcome might have differed – but do approach the discussion in such a way that she will come up with her own answers, rather than forcing her to listen to you preaching from the high ground of experience!

Action plan
How to give age-appropriate responsibilities

Allowing your child a little autonomy – appropriate to her age and developmental stage – will increase her trust in her own judgement and make her more self-reliant. However, remember that you will need to hold your child accountable, to some extent, for how well she carries out her allotted duties, or else she won't feel that you trust her fully. Do this from a positive stance, though, rather than criticizing: for example, tell her what she has done well before pointing out where she might improve next time.

Here are some suggestions, in age categories, for the kinds of responsibilities you could give your child.

Toddlers

O Let her decide what to wear – within limits and depending on the occasion.

O Give her a choice of what to eat from a selection of suitable options that you want to offer.

○ Allow her to feed herself (whenever the type of meal, time frame and situation allows).

○ Let her decide which toys she wants to share with others but also which ones she wants to keep for herself.

○ Ask her to choose which books to read with you and, similarly, which DVDs or videos to watch.

○ Allow her to pick what she wants to watch on the TV (from a choice and with a time limit set by you!).

○ Encourage her to clean up minor spillages – endorsing the message that we must all help around the house.

○ Let her decide where she wants to keep things in her bedroom.

○ Hand over to her the decision for the order of the bed-time routine – pyjamas first or ablutions?

○ Give her a say in which foods to buy at the supermarket, with you giving 'either/or' choices.

Pre-school children

○ Encourage her to decide which clothes can be put away or into the dirty laundry bag.

○ Let her decide what to wear.

○ Ask her to tidy her room to a pre-agreed standard (which may require an element of compromise on your part!).

○ Get her to decide which of her posters/artworks to display and where they should go in the house.

○ Give her the option of asking friends over to play.

○ Let her choose whether you should go to the play park or swimming.

○ Let her tell you how she wants to wear her hair.

○ Allow her the choice of having bubbles in the bath or not.

○ Ask her what she would like to write (or have written for her) in greetings cards.

○ Let her choose whether she would like to accept or decline party invitations.

Infant-school age

○ Allow her to choose her friends.

○ Let her decide which books she would like to borrow from the local library.

○ Ask her what she would like you to include in her school lunchbox (from a selection offered by you).

○ Give her the responsibility for completing her homework on time (with your gentle reminders!).

○ Allow her to pack her school bag – with supervision.

○ Let her decide which clubs and/or other activities she would like to join.

○ Get her to make simple snacks for herself or others.

○ Give her the choice of saving or spending her pocket money, after you have had a discussion about the pros and cons of each.

○ Ask her to help set and clear the table.

○ Encourage her to help you prepare a meal.

○ Suggest she makes her own cards for birthdays and other occasions.

○ Let her feed the family pets.

Junior-school age

○ Give her the responsibility for how and when to get homework done.

○ Let her help make her own lunch for school.

○ Ask her to tidy her bedroom.

○ Allow her to clean out and care for pets.

○ Encourage her to look after her own personal care: teeth cleaning, hair brushing, washing and dressing.

○ Get her to help you prepare a simple meal, such as breakfast, for example.

○ Suggest that she keeps a record of birthdays for you – perhaps on a calendar – so she can check regularly whose big day is coming up next.

○ Let her use the internet for school research (with parental controls in place, and with supervision).

○ Allow her to choose new clothes – within reason!

High-school age

○ Give her the responsibility for waking herself up for school – but be ready to get her up yourself sometimes!

○ Let her make her own packed lunch.

○ Encourage her to unload and re-stack the dishwasher.

○ Ask her to help you to keep the home tidy.

○ Let her buy gifts from her own savings.

○ Hand over the responsibility of keeping tabs on her savings account.

○ Leave it up to her to remember to practise her musical instrument.

- Ask her to make sure she puts her school uniform into the laundry basket when necessary.

- Encourage her to look after her own personal care – showering or bathing, as well as other grooming.

- Ask her to help you prepare a meal, such as a simple lunch with minimal cooking.

- Let her make an unaccompanied trip to the local shop or a friend's house: start with a three- or four-minute walk with no busy roads to cross.

What children say about self-reliance

'I couldn't believe it when my mum suddenly asked me to do the washing up. I'd never been asked to do anything grown-up before, but it was fun! Now I do it after dinner. I don't like drying up, though – only washing…'

ROLAND, 8, NEWTON ABBOT

'I'm always coming up with good ideas, my dad says. When we got our new cat, she wouldn't wear the collar with the magnet on it that worked the catflap. My mum and dad didn't know what to do, but I said why not tape the catch on the catflap down so that it didn't need the magnet to make it work, and my dad said that was a brilliant idea. I like coming up with things. I think one day I might be an inventor or something where you have to keep having good ideas.'

CARMEN, 9, BIRMINGHAM

'I always do my homework in the kitchen while Mummy is making dinner, because then I know she's there if I get stuck. But I can do most of it without asking for her help. I don't know why having Mummy there makes a difference, but it does. I think I'd be scared of going wrong if I was on my own in the other room.'

MARCUS, 7, MARKET HARBOROUGH

'My best thing to wear is my Barbie princess dress. Sometimes Mummy and Daddy let me wear it to the shops if it's not raining. I love getting dressed when I can wear my Barbie things. I don't like doing it when I have to wear proper clothes, though. I don't think Mummy and Daddy will let me wear my Barbie dress to school, so I don't really want to go.'

HANNAH, 4, DISS

Overcoming setbacks in friendship

Sometimes, even with the best will in the world, friendships come under threat – and this can be true of the strongest and most enduring of adult friendships, as well as those of childhood. It's another illustration of how friendship differs from the parent-child relationship, in that there is no unconditional affection or love – it has to be earned and nurtured, respected and reciprocated.

Almost all children will experience the ending of a friendship at some stage of their life – sometimes it happens as a natural progression, sometimes after an irreconcilable disagreement – and it can be hard for them to get over the upset. It might be that your child's association with a friend is causing you consternation: you may suspect or have evidence, for example, that he is being led into bad behaviour. So when do you sit back and let the situation resolve itself, and when do you step in and take action?

Dealing with your child's 'broken' friendship

Firstly, it's important to realize that the way children handle break-ups and reconciliations will be influenced largely by what they have witnessed within their own families, so do try to set as good an example as possible in difficult situations. This is often easier said than done, I know, but it can actually be less galling to say 'I'm sorry' or to accept your partner's apology with good grace if you know that you're doing it for your child's benefit. The same applies to making up with friends in front of your child, if the situation arises.

'Whether you actively share your own experience of having friends with your child, or not, you have to remember that as their role model, children will naturally pick up on the relationships you have with your friends,' says child psychologist, Laverne Antrobus. 'Try to identify the qualities that your different friends have and why you feel that the friendships you have are healthy ones. Talking about the strength you draw from your friendships can act as a template for your child to help him analyze and find individuals he can really trust. Don't let him be lulled into thinking that because he has a good friendship he will not have to cope with more troubled times, though. Let him know that friendships will be tested, but that true friends can survive these rocky times and, hopefully, move on.'

There are some typical scenarios that will be played out time and again in childhood, regardless of what happens at home.

It's very common to hear young children talking about having 'broken up' with each other but, serious though it may sound, it's usually nothing more than a temporary disenchantment that's all forgotten by the next day. Children often enjoy a bit of drama and can have a tendency to overstate things somewhat, especially at junior school age. (Although the particularly sensitive ones may actually

feel as though it is the end of the world when a friendship founders, so it's important that their feelings are acknowledged before you reassure them.)

It's in junior school, too, that cliques tend to form, so a child who is out of favour with a group of children, rather than just with one particular friend, can feel very left out – and even ostracized. Pre-schoolers, on the other hand, usually take minor spats in their stride and, in any case, most won't have discovered 'best friends' or cliques yet; to them, just about anyone who's willing to play is a mate, and friendships are pretty much ten a penny!

What went wrong?

The kind of things that can cause blips in formerly firm friendships range from the truly trivial, such as disagreeing over which game to play or refusing to swap a trading card, to the more challenging, such as a new, charismatic child arriving on the scene and usurping another's position. Although your child may seem devastated to the extent that you feel you should get involved and sort things out, it usually pays to wait a few days and let the dust settle; otherwise, your involvement could be seen as an acknowledgement that something really serious is going on, and the whole situation could get blown out of all proportion.

In older children, a threat to a friendship may be more significant than one amongst the younger age group. This occurs because the role of friendship takes on greater significance as children mature and older children tend to

It's hard to take a back seat when faced with a sobbing child whose world seems to have imploded, but as long as you offer your child cuddles, sympathy and support, he'll probably be able to sort things out for himself.

use their closest pals as confidants, as well as playmates. A break-up in a friendship where at least one child has disclosed intimate details about himself or his family, can leave either or both parties feeling vulnerable. However, this isn't in itself enough of a reason for you to intervene. Sometimes a friendship simply runs its course; what's important is that we teach our children that all close relationships carry an element of risk, but that it's usually a risk worth taking because of the advantages these associations bring.

It's not always upsetting to children when their friendships end, though, and often there will be no outward animosity or argument. One extensive research study conducted amongst Year 1 pupils concluded that children would often simply 'drift apart' through non-interaction or because they no longer shared common ground. It's not uncommon, either, for children in junior school gradually to move away from someone they previously considered one of their best friends, usually for the same reason. Other factors that may bring an unlamented end to an established friendship include a change of school class or a house move which puts distance between the children. In other words, proximity can be a stronger factor than compatibility in whom a young child chooses as his friends.

When three's a crowd

Parents who have had experience of their child bringing home two playmates at once can often be heard complaining about the trouble with threesomes. Families with two children can experience the same difficulty when only one of their children brings a friend home and the other sibling suddenly finds himself alone. Whilst having two children in the house, playing together and entertaining each other, can be pure joy and can give you some welcome time out for yourself, when you find yourself with three children in the house at once, one or other of them nearly always ends up feeling left out and then suddenly it becomes your problem to resolve.

My advice on such threesomes is to avoid them wherever possible! It's human instinct to pair up, so if your child must have two of his best friends round at once, see if he could bring three instead, so they could perhaps split into two pairs. If you have two children and one wants a friend home, ask one of your other child's friends at the same time. Although you'll have more on your hands in terms of numbers, it could pay dividends for maintaining harmony. If you can't work it out, try to make yourself available for your other child or find him something absorbing to do while his sibling plays with his friend.

There will be times, despite your best efforts, when you will find yourself caught in the middle of a three-way friendship – but there are things you can do to help the machinery run more smoothly.

Action plan

How to make a trio work

O Find activities that involve all the children equally: skipping with a rope, shooting basketball, a board game, arts and crafts or playing charades can be more fun with three or more players, with one player acting and two guessing.

O Give your attention to the left-out child: involve him or her in a fun activity, such as helping you to cook a batch of biscuits or doing a jigsaw puzzle. The chances are the other two will soon want to join in.

O The goal is for your child to include others without adult supervision, so teach him to feel empathy for anyone who is left out. You can discuss these feelings using books, DVDs and other media with a moral issue. A very good book for younger children, which explores friendships, cooperation and being in a gang of three is *Pumpkin Soup* by Helen Cooper (see Resources).

How disagreements can strengthen friendships

All successful human relationships are built on both agreement and disagreement. Imagine if you never disagreed with your partner or best friend: wouldn't that make for a boring, complacent – possibly even stagnant – relationship? It's only by disagreeing occasionally with our closest associates, and they with us, that we can learn more about each other's opinions, likes and dislikes and sometimes come to reconsider our own.

In fact, falling out with friends – and, more specifically, the process of making up again – is considered by some behavioural experts to be a good thing. Research has shown that although conflicts may occur, friends tend to have a special commitment to each other in the management of them – and that conflict, once it is over, can actually strengthen friendships. After all, disagreements tend to be resolved and because friendships are generally based on equality and are usually formed between children who see themselves more or less as equals, this makes it simpler in some ways for them to come to an agreement than in the less democratic relationships between parents and children.

Of course, disagreement is not the same as a furious row, and any relationship which centres around complaint and criticism is doomed to failure; there has to be a certain balance between agreement and disagreement in order for friendships to remain organic – and this is known amongst behaviourists as 'the exchange theory'.

In childhood, such conflict can help children to determine with whom they do or don't share common ground: this can be helpful when they are trying to distinguish potential friends and companions from those children with whom they are probably less compatible. If you can explain this to your child in terms he understands, he is less likely to feel threatened or overly anxious when disagreements occur; and he may even come to view them positively. You could, for instance, say something like: 'Well, that was lucky; if Josh hadn't told you that he doesn't like *Dr Who*, we might have bought him the DVD as a birthday present!' or 'If Matthew just wants to play football all the time and you don't, then why don't you find some friends who enjoy more of the things you do?'. A positive outlook will mean that these minor blips can be overcome much more quickly and easily.

When to intervene

Having said earlier that it is often best to let children try to work out their differences on their own, there are some situations in which you will need to intervene. These include those occasions where your child comes under the influence of another whose behaviour is undesirable; when your child is being teased unpleasantly; when a problem between your child and his friend seemingly cannot be resolved, or when your child is being bullied. (Bullying is dealt with at length in the next chapter.)

Sometimes a child whose behaviour is less than acceptable will try to make his best friend an accomplice to his naughty deeds, and this is most common at school age. As we've seen already, younger children don't have a great capacity for manipulative behaviour, and so the reasons for their friendships are relatively naïve. Children who try to 'recruit' others to support them in their bad behaviour usually target those who they know are keen to keep their friendship, and may use threats such as 'I won't be your friend any more' if they meet with resistance. Often the behaviour is mischievous rather than devious or destructive, but sometimes a child may be persuaded to behave in ways that have more serious consequences and which are completely out of character.

If you are lucky, your child will let you know if he is being cajoled into wrongdoing – some children cannot keep up a deception, whilst others may feel badly enough about their behaviour to confess. However, if your child is reluctant to share it with you, there are ways of detecting if this kind of problem is arising. As discussed previously, young children are usually motivated to gain their parents' approval, and a generally well-behaved child who knows he is doing wrong will often display signs that all is not well: he may be unusually quiet; you may find him reluctant to talk about his day at school; he might play out the wrongdoing using his toys; you might find he asks you questions about various misdemeanours for no apparent reason or you may even catch him out in a lie.

Point out to your child that he has a right to make his own decisions about how he behaves, who he plays with and who he chooses as his friends, and remind him that a true friend will respect his right to say 'no'.

Similar signs may become apparent in a child who is being teased persistently, or even bullied. These children commonly suffer a dramatic loss of confidence and may feel unable to tell an adult about what's happening: they may have been threatened by their tormentors into keeping quiet, or they may feel that they have somehow brought the taunts on themselves and deserve no better. This is a very sorry state of affairs, but it is also one that can be hard to detect.

If you suspect your child is suffering at the hands of another, one way of testing the water is to present a similar scenario to your child and get his 'advice' on it. You could say, for instance: 'One of the mums at school has a friend whose child was being picked on by someone who was supposed to be her friend. Don't you think that's awful? Luckily she told her mum and it all got sorted out. Have you heard of this happening at your school?'. Stress to your child that letting an adult know that bullying is going on in school is not the same as 'telling tales', which he will have been taught to think is wrong. In this case, he will be telling the truth, whereas when people 'tell tales', there is usually no evidence to support the argument in either side of the dispute. If all this yields no result but you still feel uneasy,

consider making an appointment to see your child's teacher or head teacher and asking them to keep an eye on your child. They can, in turn, ask the lunchtime supervisors to be on the alert. (For in-depth advice on handling bullying, turn to pages 136–38).

Gaining your child's trust

If your child seems out of sorts in any of the ways I have described above, and he is usually a child who is happy to share his feelings, it's time for a heart-to-heart. How you go about this is up to you: you could either initiate a quiet chat at a time when he's feeling comfortable and relaxed, or you could come at the problem from a less obvious angle. If your child is generally a good talker, pick your moment and sit him down for a cuddle and a chat. If you find it easier, start the conversation when you are doing something else at the same time, like driving in the car or washing your child's hair: some children are more comfortable when there is no direct eye contact.

Sometimes bedtime can turn into a bit of a confessional session, so you might find that this is the ideal moment to start your chat.

You could start by simply asking your child if he's happy and then broaden the conversation to talk about the qualities he most admires in his friends, and those that he doesn't think are so good. Hopefully, he will open up and begin to tell you about what's been going on – especially if he is feeling uncomfortable about it. He might get you to promise not to intervene before he confides in you, of course, but you can counter this by saying that you won't take any action without his approval. If you do feel the need to do something as a result of your chat, try to leave some space before you announce this to your child, then present your plan in such a way that he can see the benefits of it to himself and his friendship.

If you feel that your child will back away if you try to approach the situation directly, you could use the same tactic of asking him his advice on a situation that 'a friend's' child has found himself in. Say, for example: 'One of my friends told me that her little boy's best mate got him to do something really naughty because he said he wouldn't be his friend any more if he didn't. What would you do if that happened to you?'. Or you could tell him about a time in your childhood when you felt that a friendship was under threat.

If neither of these approaches get a result, you might try saying that you've noticed he's not been quite himself, that you're worried he might be in some trouble and that nothing he tells you will ever stop you from loving him or get him into more trouble. Don't push it, though: it may be that if you leave the conversation at that, so that he knows you are willing to listen to him, then he'll come round to talking to you later when he feels ready to do so.

One more avenue to try is to talk to the other child's parents about whether or not they have noticed anything unusual going on between the two children. If you're uncomfortable about questioning them directly about their own child's behaviour, try confiding in them that you're a bit concerned about yours, and wonder whether theirs has mentioned anything that could be relevant. Perhaps you could ask them to do a bit of probing on your behalf.

Action plan

How to get your child to communicate

Problems of non-communication, or situations that result in your child's secrecy, can often be avoided if you set out to create good lines of communication within your family from early on. It's never too late to improve a situation, and here are some useful pointers.

○ Talk to your child openly about the issues that might concern him at each age and stage of his development. Revealing to your child that you know all about the kinds of things that children get up to and that most behaviours won't be a shock or surprise – even when you disapprove of them – will mean that your child is more likely to confide in you.

○ Make sure that you *don't* look or sound shocked if he does tell you something upsetting.

○ Really listen to your child. Try not to interrupt, and when he has finished telling you something, repeat it back to him so he knows you have heard and understood. (Your child:

'I'm really worried that Thomas isn't going to play with me any more because he's started going off with Rhys all the time and I'm not sure we're still friends.' You: 'So you think Thomas might prefer Rhys? I can understand why you might feel upset about that.')

o Use open questions like: 'What did you do with your friends today?', which encourage discussion, rather than closed questions like: 'Have you enjoyed your day?', which will almost always yield one-word answers.

o Talk to your child about peer pressure as soon as you notice it starting to come into play, and discuss how he might say 'no' if he is uncomfortable with a situation.

o Teach your child that if he is asked to do something that he knows is wrong, he will be a better friend if he tries to persuade the other child to do the right thing than if he goes along with the unacceptable behaviour.

o Try not to criticize your child's friends – this is likely to result in them banding together even more against a common enemy: you!

o Encourage the friendships that bring out the best in your child in any way you can, and persuade him to join out-of-school groups and clubs so that he can broaden his group of friends. He is less likely to bow to peer pressure if he knows he has other groups of mates to turn to.

o Don't jump down your child's throat if you disagree with how he's handling a tricky friendship: discuss things calmly and sympathetically and gently steer him towards a more acceptable attitude.

How to respond to a confession

If you are lucky enough to have a child who would rather confess to a misdeed than keep it to himself, the way you handle the information will be critical to whether or not he chooses to be honest on another occasion. Obviously, you will want him to know that you don't approve of what he's done, but equally you must praise him for being open with you, so that he feels able to do the same in the future. This mum's first-hand account of dealing with deviousness is a good illustration of this.

'Megan came home from school one day, happy and chatty as usual, but when she opened her school bag, she suddenly gasped and said "Oh, Mummy! You're going to be so cross with me!". She pulled out a short length of plastic tubing, which was apparently part of a broken toy that had been on display at the summer fete. Then she told me that her best friend, Maddie, had persuaded her to take it, and Maddie had taken the other piece so they could play with them together. Megan said she knew this was wrong, but that the toy was broken anyway, so no one would have wanted it – and Maddie had said that if Megan didn't take it she'd go off and play with someone else instead. By the time she'd finished telling me this, Megan was beside herself with remorse.

First, I thanked Megan for telling me and gave her a big hug. Then I gently explained that taking something that is for sale is actually stealing, and that it didn't matter whether the toy was broken or not, what she had done was wrong.

I asked her how she thought she could put things right, then once we'd talked about it we agreed that she would go into school with some money from her piggy bank and give it to her teacher. I thought it would be okay to tell the teacher that she had simply forgotten to pay for it, as she'd already learned her lesson and been brave enough to tell me.

Just as I thought would happen, the teacher held Megan up as a shining example of honesty to the rest of the class – which, of course, made her feel awful, and this was a punishment in itself. The next day, I mentioned to Maddie's mum that our daughters were becoming somewhat "light-fingered", and told her the tale. She was unaware of the incident, and it seemed that Maddie had had no intention of confessing. Consequently, her punishment was worse. It was a real morality tale for Megan, but the bottom line is that she knows whatever she does, as long as she tells me, I can help her to make it right.'

CORINNE, MUM TO MEGAN, 8

Moving towards resolution

Reaching a resolution to a childhood break-up doesn't necessarily mean that the children are reunited (although this is one way of bringing the situation to a satisfactory conclusion); it can also involve simply finding ways to help your child to get over the split.

If your child is keen on reconciliation, and the other child seems willing, it shouldn't be too hard to get them back on

track, though. Teach your child about empathy by asking him to imagine how his friend is feeling about things; what would make him feel better if he were in his friend's situation and what is likely to make him feel better himself. Often the answers to these three questions will have an element of crossover and you will be able to help him find a solution that will make both parties happy. It might mean asking the other child over for tea for an exclusive one-to-one play session; it might mean your child making a simple card or writing a note to his friend; it could mean you bringing the two together in the school playground and encouraging them to shake hands with each other.

If one or other child is not keen to rekindle the friendship, however, you'll need to find a way of comforting your child. Help him to express his feelings fully, and don't be afraid to baby him a little: even adolescents sometimes need to experience a little regression therapy in the form of hugs, kisses and a return to more babyish pleasures, as they struggle to get to grips with the seemingly overwhelming challenges that lie ahead. Encourage your child to build up other friendships: perhaps he'd like to invite two or three mates over at the weekend, so that he doesn't risk being rejected by just one child; perhaps you could find out from other mums what clubs or activities their children take part in and see if your child would like to join; give him more of your time and attention in the weeks following the split so that he feels loved, supported and reaffirmed, and take steps to rebuild his self-esteem (see page 162–5).

If your child seems to be involved in disputes frequently, help him to forward-plan to assert himself in a way that leaves him feeling confident that he has put his point across. He should come away feeling that he hasn't taken on any more of the 'blame' than he deserves. The important thing is that he and the other child have each been listened to, and that their points of view have been taken seriously – even if the end result is that they agree to disagree.

Finally, reassure your child that a friendship that has deteriorated isn't necessarily over forever; sometimes people pick up with old friends again later on, and he may find that his former mate comes back into his life sooner than he thinks.

What to do if the dispute happens in your home

Sometimes things can go wrong when a child comes to your home to play with your child, and this can be very awkward. You may feel uncomfortable about disciplining the visiting child – and, in any case, it can be hard to know who's done what or who started it!

Firstly, do bear in mind that when a child misbehaves in your home it could just as easily have been your child in someone else's home – and react accordingly. How would you like another child's parent to approach your child in the case of a dispute? Arguably the best way of trying for a reconciliation without either child losing face is to treat

them equally fairly – but also ultimately to get them to do the work.

Action plan

How to help children find a resolution

○ Bring the two children together in a family room (in neutral territory – not your child's bedroom).

○ Listen to your child's version of events first, because if you prevent him from speaking before the other child it will undermine his position with you. Then let the visiting child say his piece.

○ Make sure that neither child interrupts the other: reassure him that his turn will come, and that he too will be allowed to speak without interruption.

○ If either child interrupts, tell him you will keep starting over until he stops butting in.

○ Whatever you are told by either child, when he has finished speaking, ask him what he thinks he can do about the situation: this will empower him to find a way out without losing face.

○ If they cannot seem to come to a conclusion, offer them a few alternatives to vote on, and go with the most popular one. You could, for example, suggest that they shake hands and move on, or you could try a distraction technique – for example, simply putting on a favourite DVD in the living room so that they can choose to sit together without having to interact.

○ Failing a successful reconciliation, give them both a few

minutes time out in separate 'neutral' rooms, then bring them together with a diversionary activity, such as a board game, a kickabout in the garden or a TV show that you can all enjoy.

Children on breaking up and making up

'Me and my friends are always falling out, usually about what games we all want to play in the playground. It doesn't matter, though, because we've all got other friends. Usually we're back to normal after a day; sometimes we're friends again by lunchtime! My best mate out of school is called Jamie and we've been friends since we were born. I think we'll always be good friends because we like the same stuff – but we do argue sometimes.'

DANIEL, 8, CHELTENHAM

'Sometimes I wish I was a boy because they always seem to have fun together without arguing, but me and my friends are always breaking up. Once some of the girls in my group wouldn't talk to me because I said I didn't like a TV channel they were all into. I wasn't upset, even though it was me they were cross with, but two of them started crying like babies and going off into sulks, then everyone crowded around them, which was pathetic! Boys would never do that sort of thing.'

ELENA, 10, CHRISTCHURCH

'In our school, if you break up with someone and the teacher sees, you have to make up again in front of the whole class, which is so embarrassing. It's better to just stay friends – or to break up in the toilets or something, where the teacher won't see you. It doesn't always mean you don't want to be friends, just because you break up with someone. Sometimes it just means you're a bit bored with them. Me and my mates usually make up the same day if we have an argument.'

RORY, 7, ABERDEEN

'I don't like Katy any more because she broke my dolly. Mummy says I shouldn't have taken it to playgroup but I wanted to. I liked Katy before, but people who break your dollies aren't very nice. If she buys me a new dolly I might like her again.'

ESTHER, JUST 4, NEWCASTLE

How to recognize and combat bullying

Experts don't all agree on what constitutes bullying: some believe that a single incident, such as giving another child a rough shove in the playground, can be called bullying; others assert that bullying implies a sustained campaign of unpleasant behaviour towards an individual.

Whatever your own personal beliefs about bullying, it's important to note that many children will be upset after just one isolated attack and, according to the children's charity ChildLine, will even make contact for advice and support as a result. While some experts may not agree that one single incident constitutes bullying, most concur about the types of behaviour that it commonly features.

What constitutes bullying?

The child, or group of children, who bullies another is often doing so as a way of exerting power over a victim – usually someone targeted for her vulnerability. Bullying behaviour usually includes one or more of the following:

- Verbal abuse: including persistent taunting and aggressive name-calling.
- Sending abusive text messages, emails and instant messaging.
- Ritual humiliation or taunting of the victim.
- Intentional exclusion and isolation of the victim (effectively 'sending her to Coventry').
- Physical attacks; especially when the victim is alone or otherwise vulnerable.

- Threatening or menacing behaviour – including black-mail or forcing the victim to do things against her will for fear of reprisal.
- Damaging the victim's possessions.
- Spreading malicious rumours or lying about the victim.
- Stealing or demanding money from the victim.

Why are some children bullied and not others?

This is a tricky question, and one that parents often ask themselves. Sometimes the bully's target has an obvious Achilles' heel: she may have a physical disability or other point of difference (such as an unpopular hair colour; wears glasses; is overweight, underweight, very short or very tall); the bullying may be racist in nature or concern a child's religious beliefs; or the victim may simply appear vulnerable to the bully.

However, there are many occasions when bullying occurs for no apparent reason. Bright, attractive children can just as easily fall victim to bullies as those with visible disadvantages – in fact, according to the director of Kidscape, Michele Elliott, a charity which supports bullied children and their families, this is often the case. According to her, 'In my experience most victims are sensitive, intelligent, gentle children. They don't come from a home full of conflict and shouting, so when a bully comes at them they don't know quite what to do'.

How common is bullying?

According to the results of the National Bullying Survey 2006, 69 per cent of the 4,772 schoolchildren (aged five and upwards) who took part complained that they had been bullied, with all respondents claiming to have suffered an average of six different types of bullying at school.

○ Name-calling was the most frequently cited form; 56 per cent of the abusive remarks made reference to the child's weight or appearance.

○ More than 50 per cent of pupils said they had been physically hurt, with 34 per cent of those needing professional medical attention as a result.

○ Most in-school bullying (30 per cent) took place in the playground; 25 per cent happened in the classroom; 21 per cent in the corridors; 14 per cent in the lunch queue and 7 per cent in the toilets.

○ As a result of bullying, 61 per cent of pupils said they were sometimes afraid to leave their homes.

○ 30 per cent of children who had been bullied said they had felt suicidal as a result.

○ Among the parents who were surveyed, 87 per cent claimed their child had been bullied in the last year. Most (77 per cent) were aware of more than five attacks.

WITH THANKS TO BULLYING ONLINE, THE CHARITY THAT RAN THE SURVEY AND WHICH PROVIDES VALUABLE ONLINE SUPPORT (WWW.BULLYING.CO.UK).

Additionally, the bully is frequently someone whom the victim once held in high regard: ChildLine research revealed recently that as many as 20 per cent of the bullied children who use the service cite their bullies as being former friends.

Why some children bully

Bullies are, quite often, children (and adults) who suffer from low self-esteem. A bully's behaviour may in fact be a reaction to a bad or disrupted home life, a bereavement or other loss, or parental divorce or separation; it might also occur as compensation for what she perceives to be her own inadequacies – or it may even remain unexplained. Bullying behaviour can sometimes gain the bully the fear or admiration of her peers, and this in turn can increase her feelings of power and, therefore, self-esteem. So it's clear to see that some children who bully may be damaged individuals who need help themselves.

For some children, bullying is simply passing behaviour down the line; the perpetrator may well have experienced being bullied herself – either by peers, parents, relatives or other individuals – or she may have witnessed one or other of her parents being bullied. It's well known that most of a young child's behaviour patterns, both good and bad, are learned at home; whether it is by observing what is going on in front of her within her family group, or as a result of being exposed to violent media or other materials at

home, or because she is frequently left with unsupervised and unregulated access to the internet. Whatever the reason behind the behaviour, it is important that parents and carers make clear to their children that bullying in any form is not acceptable.

What are the signs that your child is being bullied?

There is no way to know for sure if your child is being bullied, unless she tells you so herself – and, sadly, victims of bullying are often too cowed, fearful of reprisals or ashamed of their perceived 'weakness' to tell anyone what is going on. If you see any of the following behaviour in your child, though, it is worth delving a little deeper to find out what is going on. So take action if your child:

○ comes home with missing or damaged clothing or other property.

○ seems short of money at the end of the day or week at school.

○ has unexplained scratches, bruises or other injuries (although many bullies will ensure that injuries are not easily spotted by targeting places which are usually covered by clothing).

○ suddenly finds schoolwork difficult or challenging.

○ has trouble concentrating.

○ seems distant from people to whom she has previously been close.

o regularly pleads that she is ill in a bid to skip school (although give this one a little more time just in case it is genuine and your child is suffering with something).

o starts to talk about herself in a negative way or by using derisory terms.

o appears more irritable, upset or emotional than usual.

o uses a different route to and from school (this one is

If your child's friend is a victim

It can also be hard to be the friend of someone who is being bullied, as child psychologist Laverne Antrobus explains: 'Bullying is one of the most complex and multi-layered issues a child may come across. It can leave everyone feeling exposed: the person being bullied feels isolated and those around her can feel under pressure to keep their distance because they do not want to be subjected to the same treatment. Issues of loyalty will be tested in such situations; even the most robust children will need help to stand by the victim. Parents of a bullied child's friends can help by talking to their children about the importance of adhering to their principles and by helping them to test their skills of empathy. Ask your child to put herself in her friend's shoes and think how she would want her to react if she was the one being bullied. By getting her to think in this way, you will be reminding her that the decisions she makes can have an impact on her friendships.'

more applicable to older children who travel to school without you).

○ talks about suicide, either directly or in obscure terms.

Action plan
How to deal with bullying

○ If a child tells you that she is being bullied, take it very seriously. Don't just assume that the behaviour she is describing is simply playground in-fighting – and, above all, don't tell her that it's all part of growing up or that she has to learn to 'fight back'. As we have seen, bullying leads to a loss of confidence and self-esteem – and in some situations even to thoughts of suicide (which, in some extreme cases, can be acted upon).

○ Impress upon your child that it is not in any way her fault that she is being bullied.

○ Think about how you would feel if you were being intimidated, threatened or physically abused at work. No child should ever be expected to endure suffering at the hands of another – whether physically or emotionally.

○ Remember, it will have taken your child a lot of courage to tell you about the bullying in the first place, and she needs to know that you will be on her side, ready to fight her corner and help her to sort things out.

○ If you suspect that your child may be the victim of bullying but she is not willing to say so, do your best to find out the truth. Ask her friends and their parents; could another adult or a teacher talk to her and get her to open up?

○ Talk to your child in general terms about ChildLine, which is a support group specifically for children. Tell her that all children should know that there is a confidential service for bullied children, and give her the telephone number on the pretext that she might want to share it with anyone she knows who may be being bullied.

○ Don't approach your child's teacher or the school head teacher without her approval; in fact, don't take any action at all without her agreement. She may be very scared of reprisals – in some cases justifiably so. Instead, talk to her about what she thinks she would like to do next to address the problem.

○ Encourage your child to keep a record of the bullying incidents, including dates, times and the names of any children involved. This way, if you do decide to approach the school, you will have evidence to present up front.

○ With your child's agreement, make an appointment for her (and you, if she's willing for you to be there) to give her side to a teacher she feels at ease with.

○ To deal with bullying effectively, all school staff, parents and children must be involved. The school should adopt a zero-tolerance policy and should be able to provide evidence that this is being adhered to.

○ Be persistent. Some schools are resistant to admitting there is a bullying problem in the school: even if they do accept that the problem exists, it can take time and repeated negotiations on your behalf to get it tackled head on.

○ If you are not getting appropriate support from the

school, write a formal letter to the Board of Governors (the School Boards in Scotland). If you feel strongly that the school is turning its back on the problem, you can contact your local education authority.

○ Heap praise on your child and reassure her every day that you love her. She will be feeling very short of self-esteem and confidence, and will need your loving support more than anything.

○ Outside of school hours, don't let your child dwell on bullying; instead, engage her in enjoyable, relaxing activities to make home life as positive and happy as possible.

(ADAPTED FROM CHILDLINE'S INFORMATION LEAFLET *BULLYING: WHAT CAN PARENTS DO?*. FOR MORE HELP AND ADVICE ON BULLYING AND OTHER CHILD-RELATED ISSUES CONTACT CHILDLINE. SEE RESOURCES FOR CONTACT DETAILS.)

If you suspect your own child is a bully

It's not uncommon for one child to bully another in a one-off incident, and this is usually dealt with swiftly by parental admonishment or other punishment. Sometimes, though, a child may be an occasional but regular bully, or she may carry out a spate of bullying which is short-lived, but intense. So what can make a normally well-mannered child turn to bullying?

Often, children who bully are either seeking attention, are under some kind of stress or are passing bullying down the line – in other words, they are being bullied themselves.

Before you leap to conclusions, though, the best thing to do is to talk to your child about possible triggers; decide on a course of action that might break the pattern (see Action plan, below) and discuss with her how she will atone for her behaviour and help her to change.

It sounds easy, but it isn't. However, following the action plan below – and, most importantly, sticking to it – should bring results. If not, it may be worth seeking a referral from your GP to a family therapist or behaviourist, who should be able to get to the bottom of the behaviour and instigate a change.

Action plan
How to stop your child bullying

o Firstly, remain calm and in control when you discuss possible triggers with your child. Is she in need of more of your time? Is there a new baby on the scene who is deflecting attention away from her? Is she finding schoolwork difficult? Has she been bullied herself? Has there been a family bereavement or a house move which has unsettled her? Has someone said something to her that has touched a raw nerve and provoked her to retaliate? Is she simply bored? Try not to react if she turns on you or blames you: like a cornered animal, she'll be looking for a way out.

o Ask her for a full account of the circumstances surrounding her behaviour. Who else was involved? Why did she target her victim?

o Talk to your child about how being bullied must feel, and

about the long-term emotional impact such behaviour can have on victims.

O Meet with your child's victim and her family, and explain to your child that it is only by apologizing unreservedly for her behaviour that she will be able to move on and change for the better.

O Enlist the help of school staff – including lunchtime supervisors – in monitoring your child and others.

O Stress to her that this sort of behaviour will not be tolerated and any repetition of it will be punished by a significant withdrawal of privileges. (It is up to you to decide what these might be.)

O Reach agreement with her that her behaviour will change, and give her an incentive such as a reward or treat if she manages to stay out of trouble for a pre-set period of time. But make it clear that there must be no return to the behaviour after this time or there will be some sort of consequence.

O Help your child to find other strategies for dealing with her frustration or anger: taking herself off somewhere quiet for five minutes until she has cooled down; talking to another child who is willing to support her in changing her behaviour; taking deep, regular breaths and concentrating only on her breathing for some minutes.

O Don't forget to praise your child for good behaviour, and do let her know when you have noticed her behaviour changing for the better.

Did you know?

Research carried out for the NSPCC found the following:

○ Children who were abused or neglected by their parents were more likely than others to experience bullying, discrimination, or being made to feel different by their peers.

○ A quarter of adults who had been bullied by their peers in childhood reported that they suffered long-term harmful effects.

○ Research for ChildLine and the Department for Children, Schools and Families (DCSF) found that just over half (54 per cent) of both primary and secondary school children thought that bullying was 'a big problem' or 'quite a big problem' in their school; 15 per cent of primary school students, and 12 per cent of secondary school students said that they had bullied other children and been bullied themselves in the last year.

○ Around a third of boys (35 per cent) and a quarter of girls (26 per cent) admitted they had bullied other children 'a little' and/or 'a lot'.

○ Research involving 2,300 pupils aged 10–14 from schools across England found that 30 per cent of these children did not tell anyone that they had been bullied. This percentage was higher for boys and older children.

What children say about bullying

'I used to be a bit of a bully, but I think it was because I had been bullied myself at junior school. It's hard to put up with being bullied, and part of you thinks that if you turn mean yourself, people will stop picking on you. I'm ashamed of what I did, and now that I'm at high school, I've stopped bullying. There is a zero-tolerance policy at my school, so my parents would definitely find out if I did anything wrong. Anyway, I don't want to do it any more because I know what it feels like to be the person being bullied. I'm going to volunteer to be a mentor for people who are bullied when I get into Year 9. They help the smaller kids deal with bullying and go with them to report it.'

NIALL, 11, GOSPORT

'I was too afraid to tell my mum and dad when I was being bullied because I knew they would go and see some of the bullies' parents and then I'd have been in worse trouble. I wasn't physically hurt, but my whole group of friends ignored me and wouldn't talk to me or look at me just because I didn't want to do something bad they had planned. It was really unfair that they punished me for doing the right thing, and I kept thinking that if they hurt me instead of ignoring me at least it would be over with quickly. If I had told the teachers what was going on I would have got them all into trouble, and I was scared that they might do worse things to me. In the end I got in with a different group of

kids, and they're much nicer to me and don't get into any trouble. Now it doesn't matter if the others speak to me or not, although it's still not very nice being ignored.'

ANNA, 10, MIDLOTHIAN

'Big kids pushing little kids around in the playground isn't nice. Some kids only do it when the teacher isn't looking, then they say they didn't do it. Sometimes people get hurt, but they don't say anything to the teacher because they're frightened that the big kids will come after them after school. I think it's like bullying, which the teachers say is wrong. Our school has posters up telling people they mustn't be bullies, but some people still do it anyway. If anyone did it to me I'd be scared, but I'd still tell my teacher and my dad.'

SANDEEP, 8, BOLTON

'My class did an assembly on bullying, and I didn't like even pretending to be mean to my friends. You could feel what it would be like just by acting it out. I think we all learnt a lot from rehearsing and doing the assembly. I hope other kids in the school got a good message too. Bullying shouldn't ever happen to anyone. I don't understand why people do it. It's about the nastiest thing you can do to someone. My dad says grown-ups bully other people, too. If that's true, I hope I don't get bullied when I'm grown up.'

MAURA, 9, CO. ANTRIM

'I had to move schools because the bullying was so bad. I'd only been there two terms but I couldn't stand it any more. I was bullied for having red hair, which isn't my fault, and other kids were getting kicked and hit just for not being very good at sports or being a bit overweight. I don't ever want to see the girls who were bullying me again. Luckily, my new school is close to where I live, whereas the first school was on the other side of town, so I'm not too likely to bump into any of them. What made me really scared was that the teachers kept saying they were keeping an eye on the bullies, but it was still going on. I think the teachers just don't really know what to do, and the bullies are clever because they only attack people when there aren't any teachers around, and then they all stick up for each other saying they weren't even there. It was a total nightmare and I never want to go through it again. I'm so glad my mum and dad believed me and moved me to another school. It's not such a good school academically, but I can work better because I feel safer and happier.'

ROSE-ANNE, 11, BILLERICAY

What teachers say about bullying

'In my experience, the provision of out-of-school clubs effectively reduces bullying in the playgrounds as pupils are more positively employed in the clubs and are focused on what they will do when they get there. Activities in the clubs are mostly non-academic, too, so those children who bully out of a sense of inferiority in the classroom get a chance to excel at something that isn't based on formal learning.'

ANNA, YEAR 5 JUNIOR-SCHOOL TEACHER

'We can only know about bullying if we are told about it – and so much of what we do hear is one child's word against another's. The real way forward is to educate the children – and their families – about the effects of bullying on all concerned.'

GILLIAN, YEAR 7 TUTOR, MIXED COMPREHENSIVE

'Last year we were experiencing higher levels of bullying than in previous years, so we got all the pupils together, year by year, in the school gym and provided each individual with a piece of paper and a pencil, then asked them to write down their best ideas for stopping bullying. Since then, the bullying rate has dropped dramatically – in fact, I don't think we've had more than one or two cases since. Bringing the concept to the forefront of each child's mind seems to have effected a kind of sea change.'

MARCUS, HEAD TEACHER, ALL-BOYS' GRAMMAR SCHOOL

Rebuilding confidence after a crisis

Confidence is not a constant in anyone's life. It waxes and wanes depending on our circumstances; how different life events affect us; our choice of partner or friends; their choice or rejection of us and also our successes or our perceived failures. Confidence – especially self-confidence – is, however, one of those things that is very easy to lose, but equally hard to regain.

The wrong word said to a growing child at the wrong time can destroy his self-confidence in an instant.

Domestic upheavals, problems at school and minor failures can all have lasting, damaging effects if they are handled insensitively. A child who suffers a real crisis of confidence as a result of a specific event, or series of events, is in danger of developing negative character traits – and these may stay with him long after the crisis seems to have passed. That is, of course, unless some action is taken to help him come to terms with the situation and rebuild that all-important confidence.

Loss of confidence in young children

Little children are often the butt of (usually well-meant) jokes amongst adults and older children. This happens for a number of reasons, one of which is that they are an easy target, being vulnerable and naïve, which means an older child can raise his self-esteem without too much effort by teasing them; another is that jokes at their expense quite often go over their heads. However, another more common reason is that youngsters very often say and do things that are wonderfully funny – usually without realizing it. When a child with limited language skills gets something wrong in conversation, for instance, it's a natural response to want to share his error with others, simply because it sounds funny or cute. But this can backfire with dramatic consequences.

A friend's five-year-old, for instance, asked her big brother to 'play giraffes' with her. He dismissed her request somewhat sarcastically, saying 'I don't know what you're on about. How do you play *giraffes*?'. It was only when she got the chequerboard and counters out that he realized she was asking him to play *draughts* with her. His immediate reaction was to burst out laughing and relate the story to the rest of the family. His little sister, meanwhile, had put the game away and taken herself off to her room sobbing. It had been the latest in a string of similar incidents, and it proved to be the final straw: his little sister refused to speak in front of him for several days afterwards, and the development of her vocabulary took a temporary and undesirable downward slide.

This sort of scenario occurs commonly, and so easily – and the irony is that in such situations we are usually laughing out of a sense of endearment, not mockery. Certainly, this little girl's brother would never have knocked

his sister's confidence intentionally, and yet her formerly outgoing, confident nature was lost for a while after he related to the rest of his family what he thought was a charming and amusing episode. This story does illustrate, though, how important it is to avoid making fun of young children (however playfully) who have not yet learned to laugh at themselves, and whose efforts at learning the skills that older children take for granted will frequently result in syntax errors and other wrong-footings.

The impact that such unintentional humiliation has on the very young is illustrated by the experience of another friend's son during his first term in Reception class. Four-year-old Sam had joined the school enthusiastically; he had spent the previous term in the school nursery, where he was leaping ahead with early reading and writing skills, and he felt very grown-up and also proud to be donning a school uniform and taking a full part in life at 'big school'.

However, just a few weeks into the first term, Sam was involved in an incident with another child's toy: the other child had been passing it to Sam for him to look at when it accidentally dropped to the floor and broke. Sam was accused by the other child of deliberately breaking his toy, and the teacher chose to believe him. She demanded that Sam apologize, but he refused, saying that he wasn't going to say sorry because he'd done nothing wrong (thereby demonstrating an admirable sense of justice, you could argue!). He ended up being punished for his alleged 'crime' by being made to stand in a corner of the playground by himself, crying, for the entire lunch break. By the end of break he had made his mind up that he no longer enjoyed school and didn't want to go there any more.

Lasting effects of humiliation

Of course, humiliation doesn't only have an adverse effect on the younger age group: in older children, as well as in adults, it's one of the greatest causes of plummeting self-esteem. This is particularly true if we fail suddenly in an area where we previously succeeded: for example, if a child who has become proficient and confident at swimming is picked out to demonstrate a stroke to the other children, then he bungles it and ends up being laughed at. In such a situation, humiliation can take its toll – even to the extent that a formerly strong swimmer may give up his sport rather than risk embarrassment a second time.

To put this into context, consider how you, as an adult, would feel if one of your greatest skills was suddenly undermined or unexpectedly deserted you. You may, for example, have talked a group of friends into allowing you to coach them on a skiing trip because you are known as a formidable skier: imagine then arriving in the resort and finding yourself unable to tackle the simplest runs without falling over. Chances are you will be in no hurry to repeat the trip – or your boasts about your skills – any time soon!

My friend had a great deal of trouble rebuilding Sam's enthusiasm for school, which didn't return fully until he was in Year 1 with a new teacher. If the situation had been better handled by the Reception teacher, Sam might not have had his enthusiasm for school so dented. The teacher might have had a happier result if she had examined all the evidence before leaping in and punishing poor Sam – this was a genuine accident which could have been sorted out in minutes – or she simply could have discussed the incident with the children's mums after school and asked them how they would like to handle it. In any case, the punishment meted out to this formerly confident and outgoing youngster did not seem to fit the perceived 'crime' or the child's age, and it ended up being ultimately counter-productive in affecting Sam's happiness at school.

Other reasons for loss of confidence

There are many, many reasons why children may suffer a loss of confidence – and some of them may happen without us noticing. Perhaps, as above, a teacher has made an example of your child for something he didn't do, or maybe your child's granny has mistaken his best portrait of her for a picture of a rocket ship. An incident like one of these may seem to us adults to pass by in a whisper, but a vulnerable child may dwell on his unarticulated hurt feelings for a long time afterwards. By the time you come to ask your child what has upset him, he may not even be able to recall the incident, but the damage will already have been done.

When we get it wrong

There are times when, with the best will in the world, we parents can be the cause of our children's setbacks. Being a parent is a 24-hour job, and no one can be expected to behave impeccably all the time – and that goes for how we respond to our children, too. If you have ever said something spiteful to your child in retaliation for his bad behaviour, or uttered something sarcastic and hurtful because you have been wound up beyond your limit, you might feel that you would give anything to turn back the clock and erase the moment from your child's memory.

Hopefully these episodes are few and far between, if they happen at all, but if they do occur the only way of restoring your child's confidence is to acknowledge that you were wholly in the wrong. It's no good saying: 'Well, I'm sorry I said that, but you were driving me mad!' (In other words: 'It was your fault – you brought it on yourself'). No, you need to apologize wholeheartedly and unreservedly, however small it may make you feel. You should also reassure your child that what you said was not meant.

Sometimes the cause can be more obvious, though: if, for instance, your child has not been picked for the school football team; if he lets his side down during a match by missing an important pass or failing to score a critical goal; if he is publicly moved down a group in maths; if he has

recently been diagnosed with a learning disorder or if he has been bullied (see Chapter 6), you can expect to see in him a loss of confidence and you will need to equip yourself to start boosting his self-esteem once more.

Children's reactions to let-downs, humiliation and embarrassment are often more dramatic than those of adults because their confidence is still in the process of being built up, and so is fragile and often untested. Because of this, it helps if adults can be aware of potential crises, so try to spot the signs that your child's confidence has taken a knock, then make sure you take steps to help him over it.

Bereavement and divorce

The link between bereavement and/or divorce or separation and your child's confidence may be less obvious to spot than in the situations described above, but they can really knock a child for six.

Your child is most likely to have believed, at least until around junior-school age, that marriages, partnerships and all the important relationships around him go on for ever – and he has probably felt quite confident about this. So if he suddenly finds himself bereaved or in the midst of a family break-up, he will almost certainly begin to mistrust his own judgement about such things. He may even think

Children are not fools: even quite young children will sense if you are not being honest with them.

that he has done something to cause the death or divorce, so his confidence in himself as a worthwhile human being will be under threat. At the same time, he will be struggling to come to accept and understand what has happened.

A truthful approach will be most helpful to your child: it's pointless telling your child, for example, that Grandad has 'gone to sleep and won't wake up any more' or has 'moved in with the angels' when you actually mean that he has died. Both explanations could leave your child confused, fearful and upset.

In the first instance, why is Grandad suddenly unable to be woken up, when he has always awoken quite healthily from sleep before? This may set up a deep-seated fear in your child of going to sleep himself – or of anyone else close to him sleeping. When my own mum died suddenly, I explained to my daughter, who was then almost five, that Grandma had fallen asleep in her armchair and died while she slept (which was true). I thought, in my own distress, that this would allow Natasha to imagine that Grandma hadn't suffered. Instead she became paranoid about me dozing off, convinced that if this could happen to Grandma, who had just the day before been enjoying tea with us in the garden, it could certainly happen to me, too. It took an awfully long time for the association to be lost.

If you opt for the second explanation, your child might wonder why Grandad would rather live with the angels than at home where he belongs.

In my opinion, the only reasonable way of breaking bad news to children is to be as honest as possible without being brash. You could say, for instance: 'Sadly, Grandad has died; this means we won't see him again. Of course, we'll all feel very upset about this for some time, but eventually we'll be able to remember him happily'. If you feel too distressed to speak to your child rationally and calmly, ask your partner or another close relative to be there to lend support, or to break the news for you.

If you have religious beliefs, then by all means say that Grandad is in heaven, but explain that he is living in a different state from when he was on earth; tell your child that Grandad's body isn't needed any more but his soul exists somewhere none of us will know until it is our turn to die.

Equally upsetting to a child can be when his parents split up. If you and your partner are separating, your child will be going through all the emotional and physical upheaval that you are yourselves. Again, try to keep your child in the picture about what is happening every step of the way, tell him that although you and your partner don't love each other enough to live together any more, the love you both have for him will never change. Reassure him often; give him extra attention, lots of hugs and opportunities to ask questions or express his feelings. If you are moving, involve him in preparing his new room in the new home, and try, for his sake, to remain on at least superficially friendly terms with your ex, so that your child doesn't feel torn in his loyalties to either of you. Difficult as it may be, do also try to avoid openly criticizing your ex or discussing him in unfavourable terms when your child is within earshot.

Explain that there are different kinds of love and that whilst grown-ups may stop loving each other, they can still love their children just as much as always.

Why you are key to rebuilding your child's confidence

Your child judges himself first and foremost by how his parents regard him and treat him – and by how you manage to transmit these feelings to him. For this reason, you are key in building, rebuilding and maintaining his confidence. Making a point of involving your child when you are trying to resolve a crisis – but without burdening him with the responsibility of it – is a great way of boosting his self-esteem. If you can handle tricky situations maturely and calmly, your child will feel reassured that, although these things may happen sometimes, happiness can return and life can regain equilibrium once more.

In the case of bereavement, including your child in making the arrangements for the funeral – for example, by letting him write his own prayer to be read aloud or choose a favourite hymn – will help him gradually to accept Grandad's death and assimilate the information. After the event, talk about Grandad, get out photographs of him and

encourage your child to express his feelings. Let him see you grieving sometimes, so that he feels confident to cry himself without fear of upsetting you further.

In such situations it can help to sit quietly and read a book with your child that explains death in terms he can understand. *Water Bugs & Dragonflies* by Doris Stickney (see Resources) is one such useful book: it includes some references to God and heaven at the back, and a prayer for children to say, but even if you don't have a faith, the story is a very useful starting point for discussion within families who believe that people live on after death. Have a look in bookshops, on websites or even in the library and you will find other very helpful books, too, that might better suit your situation.

Pile on the praise; curb the criticism

In more general terms, you can help to rebuild your child's confidence in ways that may seem subtle, but that will seep into his consciousness nonetheless. You may frequently think how sweet and kind he is, for example, or how proud you are of him, but how often do you tell him?

One of the truisms about all modern relationships is that it's easy to carp on about one another's faults, but it doesn't come as naturally to praise. Think about it: if your child spills a drink on your newly-cleaned carpet, is your inclination to go off the deep end about his carelessness? That would be a quite natural response, but it is one that is likely to lower his self-esteem. If, however, he carries his drink carefully across the room without spilling a drop, is it your automatic response to notice and praise him? Possibly not.

As parents, we must make a conscious effort to heap praise on our children. If you start doing this from baby-hood, it will become second nature to you. We must also strive to ignore less desirable behaviour and outcomes, lest we end up labelling our children as 'clumsy', 'useless', 'messy' or 'rude' – labels which can become so ingrained in a child's psyche that he will begin to live up to them sub-consciously. It might seem like a tall order – especially for those of us who operate under huge pressure every day and are on a fairly short fuse by teatime, but it's doubly important to lay off the criticism if your child is suffering a crisis of confidence. After all, the message to him will be that if the people who know him best think he's 'stupid' or worthy of ridicule, who is he to argue?

Watch, too, what you say to other people about your child. If he overhears you saying something which is less than complimentary, he is likely to believe it because you're saying it to a third party when you think he can't hear you.

It's easy to put our children down from time to time. Remarkably, many of us have a tendency to do this even when our own children are being compared favourably to less successful children; it's a way of over-compensating. For instance, I recently heard one mum, whose daughter is a champion swimmer, saying to another parent whose child was struggling with water confidence: 'Oh yes, she's good at swimming, but she's useless at every other sport!'. Not

only do I know this to be untrue, but I suspect that had her daughter heard her mum running her down, she would have been mortified – and far less keen to take part in sports!

Practising praise-giving

It may feel contrived, but by practising praising your child you'll get better at it – just as he'll gain confidence with every piece of positive feedback he receives. If you frequently deliver a happy message it will become automatic, and your child will expect to hear good things about himself.

In this way he will also begin to measure his worth and achievements favourably, and he'll start to believe all the good things you've been telling him. So say things often like: 'You're getting really good at that, aren't you?'; 'Well done – that was a brave try'; 'I really enjoy our special time together'; 'I love you' or 'You're great' – even if there isn't any particular achievement to enthuse about.

Try to stop and control yourself whenever you feel the urge to shout, berate or criticize. Count to ten and come up with a more constructive and reasonable way of correcting him. Above all, resist the urge to say 'I told you so' when things go wrong. Hard as it may be to keep your own counsel when your child ignores your advice and does things his own way with unfortunate consequences, 'I told you so' is one of the hardest things to hear; it makes your child feel stupid for having even tried whatever he was doing, and will certainly undermine his sense of self-reliance and willingness to try new things in the future.

Highlighting our own mistakes

One of the most useful lessons we can give our children when building or rebuilding their sense of self-esteem is that it is perfectly okay to make mistakes – in fact, it is an accepted and expected part of life. Point out to your child that some of the world's greatest discoveries came about by trial and error, and that if no one had ever made any mistakes we would all be much the poorer for it.

Make yourself a role model for him: try to react with equanimity when you make a mistake yourself: saying 'Well, that didn't work, did it? I'd better try it another way' is a lot more positive than belittling yourself or exploding into a rage. It reinforces the idea that making a mistake provides an opportunity to learn something and try again – an invaluable lesson for a child, who is almost bound to experience more failures than successes during the long learning process.

Listening and responding

Regularly practise active, reflective listening with your child. This means listening without interruption to any of his fears or worries, then repeating them back to him to show that you have understood and heard what he is saying. If, for example, he says 'No one likes me', don't dismiss what he is saying as rubbish, but instead say: 'So you're finding it hard to make friends. That is tough for you,' before discussing ways in which you may be able to help him find a way forward.

Do take your child's worries seriously, even if they seem unfounded or trivial to you. To him they are obviously real and they are affecting the way he feels about himself and, for this reason alone, they deserve your credence. This doesn't mean digging really deep and making a big deal out of every little anxiety – yes, sometimes you'll want to take action to help your child, but at other times all he requires is your acknowledgement of his feelings. By the same token, try not to laugh at your child. It's fine to laugh with him once he's found the humour in a situation for himself, but to do so before he is ready will only undermine his confidence.

Think before you speak and choose your words with care – it's very easy to say something without thinking and then wish you hadn't. 'You're so clumsy' or 'Don't be stupid' can slip out in an irritated moment when a vase is smashed or an innocent question is asked. Remember, too many negative remarks can cause children to believe they are useless.

Action plan
How to rebuild confidence

○ Encourage your child to focus on the positive aspects of his abilities and his life. Talk to him about the areas in which he excels. These don't have to be academic: perhaps he is really good at putting other children at their ease; he might be clever at making up games; maybe his ball skills are better than his peers' or does he have a great imagination? Kindness, consideration, patience, loyalty and obedience are all wonderful life skills that you should praise often, and of which your child should be rightly proud.

○ Remind him of past successes: dig out certificates for sports or musical achievements, for example, and photos that depict him doing something well.

○ Regularly engage your child in doing the things he's best at: the sense of achievement he feels when he does something well will give him a valuable boost.

○ Celebrate his successes: if he passes an exam or gets picked for a swimming gala, make a fuss of him. You could take him out for a pizza; invite one of his friends for a sleepover; buy him a small present; cook his favourite meal or hire a DVD he's been wanting to see: the choice of treat doesn't matter, but whatever you choose to do, make sure you keep him central to the celebration.

○ Display trophies, medals and other prizes somewhere prominent in your home, and point them out to visitors when your child is in earshot.

○ Ask your child to coach you in the things he's good at: if he is a good chess or card player, for example, get him to give you some tips on how to improve your own game. Being cast in the role of expert should give your child a surge of self-confidence.

○ Vocalize your pride in your child often: positive affirmations have been proven to raise self-esteem. Say things such as: 'I love you so much'; 'You've been very patient today'; 'I really appreciated you offering to help in the supermarket'; 'Great homework tonight!', and so on.

⦿ Remember to praise individual incidents or behaviours rather than labelling your child: if you say 'You're always such a good boy', this can in itself feel like a burden of responsibility to your child, who may think he will let you and himself down if he misbehaves.

⦿ Devote plenty of time to doing the things that make your child happiest, whatever they may be. Allow him to enjoy himself often, and don't cut short his enjoyment for trivial reasons. By indulging him in this way he will know that his happiness is valued and is a priority to you.

⦿ Be wary of criticizing your child too often: psychologists have calculated that it takes ten lots of praise to counteract the effect of just one criticism, so if you do have to correct him on something, build him up with praise beforehand and afterwards.

⦿ Don't draw unfavourable comparisons between your child and his peers or siblings.

⦿ Encourage your child to take part in physical exercise. Scientific studies have proven that taking up a sport or other physical activity can raise self-esteem, while the release of endorphins ('feel-good' hormones) that exercise brings about can increase feelings of wellbeing. Even better if your child can join a local team or other group where he will also have an opportunity to widen his circle of friends: as we have already discussed, making friends is a great confidence booster.

⦿ If your child is not keen on sport, encourage him to develop a skill which not many others will have: juggling, simple magic tricks or body popping, for example, may earn him the admiration of his peers.

○ If you are not big on routine in your home, establishing some rituals and regular, predictable events – such as enjoying a family lunch around the table at weekends – will go some way towards making your child feel secure.

○ Make more time for your child: encourage him to talk more; make an effort to play with him; get out and exercise together; and above all, don't allow him to retreat too often into the worlds of TV or computer games, as these will do nothing to nurture his confidence.

○ Having said all that, there's no need to fill his every waking moment with activities. Allow him time and space to reflect, gather his resources and move on – just make sure he knows he can always turn to you for support.

How other parents have helped their children

'Amy has always been really keen on games at school but, sadly, she's not naturally gifted when it comes to sport. This has meant that she's often been passed over when the school rounders captains have selected their teams. We've tried practising with her as a family, and it's helped a bit, but what's made a huge difference has been organizing games of rounders at the park on alternate weekends and involving her other friends who don't tend to get picked as first choice either. I give all the children chances to be team captain,

so they all get to feel what it's like to be "in charge". Now their skills are improving weekly – probably because they are playing children of more or less equal ability. It doesn't matter so much to them now that they're not sporting superstars at school – they are at weekends, which seems to matter more! Most weeks when the weather's fine the other parents bring a picnic and stay to watch, so it's turned into quite a social event for the grown-ups, too.'

DIANA, MUM TO AMY, 9, AND DAN, 6, FROM PLYMOUTH

'Leo was very slow to start reading and writing, but we assumed he'd catch up in his own time. But when he moved up to Year 3 we were advised by his teacher to have him tested for dyslexia – it turned out that he does have the condition. Getting the diagnosis was a double-edged sword: being told he had a learning difficulty was a knock to his confidence at first, and he was especially upset about being "different" from his friends. Knowing that there was a reason for his slowness, though, stopped him from feeling stupid (a label many of his peers had pinned on him, to his great distress and ours), and this raised his self-esteem a little. Now, with the extra help he has in the classroom from a learning support teacher, his skills are improving and he also seems to have a new-found enthusiasm for his school work. It's wonderful.

We've done a lot of research into Leo's condition as well as joining the British Dyslexia Association, who have been so helpful. They've given us loads of support and informa-

tion and now we feel we can help Leo much more. At home, we pay special attention to rebuilding his self-esteem by encouraging him to see himself as someone who has plenty of ability, despite his condition, rather than thinking of himself as stupid because of it.'

ANGELA, MUM TO LEO, 8, FROM NEWCASTLE

'Li-Ming was only three when her ballet teacher suggested she dance a short solo in a show. The show was quite a big affair, with tickets on sale to the public as well as parents, and I was a bit nervous for Li-Ming, but her teacher convinced me that because she was so confident in class she'd be fine. On the afternoon of the first performance my heart was in my mouth, and when it came to her solo Li-Ming just stood there crying: she was suffering from terrible stage fright and was terrified of dancing in front of an audience. Luckily, there was an understudy who could step in, but the whole experience shattered Li-Ming's confidence. Her teacher was terribly upset about it and kept apologizing for having put her forward, but that's the thing about small children – they're unpredictable! Once we'd taken the pressure off Li-Ming by saying she didn't have to do the solo at all, she was perfectly happy to take part in the rest of the show. I have reassured her that we won't agree to any more "spotlight moments" until she feels ready, and this seems to have helped her over the upset.'

NANCY, MUM TO LI-MING, 3, FROM HARPENDEN

Frequently asked questions

Confidence, and the role it plays in making and keeping friendships, is not measurable in our children, so unless they are positively exuberant at all times, we parents will still worry about their capacity to cope with various situations that life throws at them. The different scenarios and eventualities which can threaten our children's happiness, in terms of their friendships and their self-confidence, are many. So this final chapter is dedicated to a selection of issues which trouble parents most, and the most commonly asked questions about them.

Your baby and toddler

Q **I was quite friendly with the girls in my postnatal group for a while after the births of our babies, but over the past 18 months we've drifted apart. The trouble is that my little boy is now missing out on playing with other children his age. What can I do to compensate?**

A Postnatal groups serve a very useful purpose in the early days of motherhood, as you are all sharing common experiences and can offer each other support at different stages. It's not uncommon, though, for groups like this to drift apart, especially once you become more competent parents and no longer have such a strong need to compare notes. Sometimes firm friendships grow out of these groups, but just as often some mothers tend to feel that they have little in common once their children enter toddlerhood.

At this age, your child is unlikely to have forged any serious bonds with the children from your postnatal group, so you don't need to worry that he is missing specific playmates. But there are several positive steps you can take to ensure that he mixes and socializes with his peer group. Firstly, if you have a local leisure centre, make enquiries as to what mother-and-toddler groups run there: it may offer swim sessions; exercise classes; music groups; toddler gym sessions or coffee mornings that you can join in with on an ad hoc basis. Groups like this also seem to spring up in the most surprising places, such as libraries and bookshops, which often offer drop-in sessions for everyone to meet and have storytime together.

If there doesn't seem to be anything much around, you could start your own social group for mums with same-age children. You don't need to invite strangers into your home: perhaps you could organize meetings at your local coffee shop or soft-play area. See if your GP practice is willing for you to advertise on the noticeboard, and make sure you only quote an email address or mobile phone number so you don't find unexpected guests on your doorstep or get bombarded with calls to your home phone number!

Otherwise, you can meet mums with same-age children by making frequent visits at the same time of day to your local park, or you could contact other women in your situation via an online mums' network. Visit www.netmums. co.uk and register free with your local online branch for loads of ideas for social opportunities in your area.

Q **My eight-month-old baby attends a private nursery while I work two days a week. She used to love being in the company of other babies and was positively elated to be handed over to her keyworker, but just lately she has started screaming inconsolably when I go to leave. I'm worried that something has happened with another baby or child that is making her unhappy. I don't want to take her out of the nursery as I have no other option than for her to be there, but it's heartbreaking to witness. What can I do?**

A Be reassured that the majority of babies go through this perfectly normal developmental stage. It's known as 'separation anxiety' and commonly occurs from the ages of around seven to nine months. During this period, your baby may become distraught at the thought of losing sight of you. This is because, although she has made a developmental leap in that she now realizes that she is a separate entity from you, she hasn't yet learned that you can still exist even when you are out of sight. You have probably noticed that she protests loudly at home, too, when you want to leave her to fetch something from the kitchen or go to the loo, for example.

It's most unlikely that any child has upset your baby to the extent you describe, but it's worth having a word with her keyworker in any case, to discuss how you can both handle the separation anxiety. Usually all that is required is a quick, cheery goodbye from you (amidst your baby's screaming and tears!), a positive distraction and a few minutes' cuddling from the keyworker whilst your baby adjusts to your going. You may find that she begins screaming as soon as you reappear to collect her, too. This, again, is normal as she is reminded of the earlier upset – although equally she may be overjoyed to see you.

It's worth knowing, too, that in some children separation anxiety can continue until well into their second year – but the good news is that, as with when they are younger, they do frequently settle within minutes of being left. You could also wait outside the nursery for a few minutes to listen out until your child calms down. It can be very reassuring to hear how quickly most children do settle.

Your child at school

Q **My seven-year-old daughter's teachers have mixed up the classes for this new school year, and my child has found herself separated from her best friends. Three weeks in, she is bereft and lonely in her new class. How can I help her?**

A It's tricky when this happens, but there is some sense in the decision to mix up classes. In schools where this happens, the policy tends to be to socialize and integrate children as fully as possible within each year: this not only gives each child a chance to get to know all his or her year-group peers, but it also mixes up children of different ability levels and social backgrounds, giving all the children a greater sociological understanding.

Try not to worry too much about your child. She is only three weeks into the new school year and is very likely to adapt; she'll probably make new friends amongst her classmates, too. The upside is that she can now have one group of best friends she meets up with in the playground and out of school, and another within the classroom. In the meantime, stress to her that time spent in the classroom is for learning, not socializing, and that having her best friends around her may only distract her from lessons. Reassure her that you will ensure she sees these special friends often out of school hours – and make sure that you are as good as your word. Discuss the situation with her friends' parents: they may be unaware of the problems your daughter faces, as their own children might still have some of their best friends with them in class.

You could consider inviting a few of the children in her new class home for tea and a 'getting to know you' session. This will help you to get a feel for the class so you'll be able to talk with your child about who everyone is.

If after another few weeks your daughter is still unhappy, talk to her class teacher: it's very unlikely that she will move your child into her best friends' class, but she may agree to try and team your daughter up with a like-minded child or two and nurture some new friendships within the new set-up.

For the record, this same thing happened to my own child and her best friend at this stage, and ultimately she could see that she was benefiting from the arrangement.

Somewhat pragmatically, after a few weeks she announced that she was glad she wasn't with her best friend in class any more because they would only 'make each other naughty', and that playtimes were even more special now! I initiated sleepovers and after-school play sessions to keep their friendship going, and so did her friend's parents – the two girls remain inseparable.

Q **After a recent house move, my nine-year-old son is soon to join a large new school where he will not know any other children. What can I do to help him make friends?**

A First and foremost, acknowledge that your son may find things very different at his new school, and that this is bound to cause him some anxiety. It's no good telling him that everything will be just fine – this may help to assuage your own worries about moving him, but the message he will get is that you have no understanding of how he feels. Acknowledge, too, that you realize he'll miss seeing his friends in school, but (as long as you haven't moved too far away) reassure him that he can see them outside of school. Point out that because he is a likeable lad it won't be long before he has a whole new set of friends to introduce them to as well.

See if you can arrange to make a couple of visits with him to his new class before he is due to join. This will mean taking him out of his current school for a morning or after-noon, but it will certainly help him if he can be introduced

to the other pupils in advance and can see a few familiar faces on his first day. Some school head teachers are acutely aware of how important it is for children to make links with each other and may even give you a class list so you can begin to make contact with children and their families before the start of the new term.

Reassure your son that his new teacher will be experienced in helping new pupils to settle in and won't mind if you, or he, ask lots of questions. Remind him that his class teacher (or any other teacher for that matter) will be available to help him at any time. You could also find out whether the new school operates a 'buddy' system, where your son is paired with another pupil in his class or in a higher year who will show him around and help him adapt.

Finally, let your child know that it's normal to be anxious at first, but point out the benefits: a whole new set of friends; greater proximity to his new school so he'll be able to bring mates home more often; the opportunity to join after-school clubs and groups; the chance to walk to school and back (if this is the case) and also how this move will give him more valuable time at home. This is a big step both for your child and for you as a family, but the good thing is that because you will all be new to the area, you will all be sharing the experience of making new friends at the same time.

Q **My 10-year-old daughter's group of schoolfriends has started leaving her out of their social arrangements, and she's getting an inferiority complex about it. What can we do?**

A First, assess the facts: is it true that your child is being routinely ostracized or is it just that small sub groups have formed within the main group? On occasions when your child has been included in the arrangements, have all other members of the group been present? It may be that other children have also been excluded, and this could be purely because some of the children's parents have put a limit on the number of friends who can come home at once.

Try to find out if your child has fallen out recently with any member or members of the group, and whether any dispute has been resolved: perhaps one or more of the other children is holding a grudge against her because the situation has not been addressed. In this case, chat with your daughter to see if you can agree some ways to bring about a reconciliation. If you know the other children's parents well enough, consider approaching them in a non-confrontational way (but only with your daughter's agreement) to find out whether they are aware of any splits or rifts within the group. Perhaps you could agree between you to invite smaller, mixed groups of children round so that no child feels neglected at any one time.

You can use this as an opportunity to help your child to problem-solve. What would she like to happen? How can

you help her to make some changes? You may be surprised at some of the ideas young children can come up with when they have your backing.

It sounds as if most of your child's problems revolve around her social life, so see if you can help her broaden her clique of friends by encouraging her to join new groups, clubs or other activities in your local area. Discuss what she's into that she may like to pursue further. Trampolining? Learning a new racquet sport? Swimming? Girl Guides? A dance class? All of these would bring the opportunity to meet like-minded children with whom you could encourage new friendships.

Meanwhile, do your best to heap extra praise, reassurance and love on your daughter while she goes through this tricky patch. If she is developing an inferiority complex, she needs to know now, more than ever, that she is supported at home if she is to maintain her self-esteem. Remind her of all the things she is good at, and list all her best qualities, pointing out that she is far too nice a person to be left out for long, and that any group of children that genuinely does not value her friendship is not worth wanting to be a part of.

Remember that children can be very resilient. You probably don't know the half of what goes on at school in terms of unpleasantness, rivalry and arguments between friends, but your child doesn't come home every day in floods of tears about perceived slights, does she? This is because children tend to bounce back from such upsets quickly, and it's all part of their social development that they learn some resilience in these situations. The most helpful thing you can do is listen – *really* listen. Often all a child with a social problem wants is for her parents to hear what she's saying and understand how she's feeling and what she's been through. Beware of giving her too much advice on how to handle herself, as this can undermine her self-esteem.

Do all you can, then all that's left is to sit it out and see what happens. Friendships – especially amongst groups of children – tend to be organic at least until secondary school age, and your child is likely either to get back in with the same crowd or join a separate group. As long as she is otherwise reasonably happy, don't worry.

Other friendship dilemmas

Q **My four-year-old twin boys don't share the same friends, which makes it difficult when it comes to socializing – especially when one is invited to a party and the other isn't. How can I encourage them to enjoy each other's friends?**

A The simple answer is 'Why should they?'. If you had two different-age siblings, or boy/girl twins, you wouldn't expect them to share their friends, and it shouldn't be any different just because your children are the same age and sex as each other. Really, it's better to celebrate the fact that your twins are operating as individuals rather than going around joined at the hip, as some sets of twins do.

When your boys get to school, they are likely to be put into separate classes, and this will result in more individual friendships, so it's worth working around this now. Like other siblings, they're likely to have some friends in common – particularly those that are made through your own friendships. Otherwise, do what many parents of different-age siblings do, and invite a child for each of your boys, if possible, when they want friends home. If one of your boys is invited round to his friend's house, try to arrange for your other son to go to a friend's, too – or invite one of his best mates to your home instead.

Inevitably, there will be occasions when one boy is invited to a party or other social event without his brother. Don't worry too much about this: it's perfectly normal in all other family set-ups, and what's most important is how you handle the situation. Reassure the twin who isn't invited that there will be other parties and outings for him that won't include his brother; find something exciting or absorbing for him to do whilst his brother is out; devote your time and attention to him so that the time goes quickly; make a special treat together for everyone to share so that he doesn't feel left out when his brother brings a piece of birthday cake home.

There's no need to over compensate at these times, though: with your support, your child will learn to accept minor disappointments, and realize that it may be his turn to enjoy a special outing next time.

Q My five-year-old daughter always seems to be attracted to the naughtiest children in any situation. Now that she is settled at school, I'm worried that her latest best friend – who is a handful – will become a permanent fixture and hold my child back. I want to discourage this friendship, but is it right for me to interfere?

A This is the age when some 'best friendships' can become just that – enduring associations that could well stand the test of time. However, many children don't establish a really strong bond with just one particular friend until around the age of eight or nine, so you may find that your child's enthusiasm for this particular girl will wane with time.

It's not a good idea to criticize your child's choice of friends at any age, unless they are posing a serious threat to her wellbeing. Telling her she's made a bad friend will give her the message that her own judgement is not to be trusted, and this will undermine her confidence at this critical time when she's beginning to have to make some responsible decisions for herself.

If, as you say, she is always drawn to the naughty child in a group, it could be that she is envious of these children's apparent freedom of expression. Are you perhaps overly strict with her? Is there room for a little more leniency? Turning a blind eye to some aspects of her behaviour, even if they are less than desirable, is actually likely to reinforce your values; the important thing is that she has been allowed to test the boundaries in order to find this out.

Rather than discouraging particular friendships, you could try to nurture others. If there is another child you know that she plays with and seems to get along with, arrange to have this child round to play. If your child is resistant to the idea, strike up a friendship with the friend's mother and tell your child that the two of you want to get together, so you're expecting her to make the other child welcome. With any luck they will hit it off – especially if the other mum returns the favour. Don't push it, though, if they clearly don't get on.

Encourage your child to join an after-school club, if any are on offer, such as a choir, a sports club or an art class where she will meet other children in her school year. (If you want to be really sneaky, you could find out which afternoons her 'best friend' is busy, then enrol her in a group that meets on that day so that they can't join up together.) See if she would like to join the local Brownie pack, where she will eventually have the opportunity to go on pack holidays with other girls her age. These provide a great bonding environment.

If all else fails, your best course of action is to continue to set a good example yourself in terms of respecting other people; respecting property; practising good manners and conducting yourself in a way you would like to see her emulate. There is plenty of research to support the fact that a child's most important role models are her parents and other main carers. Tell her, too, that you don't mind who she is friends with as long as she doesn't follow them into bad behaviour, and that it is her job to show her friends how to be good: otherwise she will be letting her friends down as well as herself and you.

Q **My 11-year-old son always befriends the 'underdog' and seems to enjoy bossing these more vulnerable children around. It's not bullying – more like showing off – but it makes me feel uncomfortable nonetheless. Is there a way of encouraging him to forge more balanced friendships?**

A Children who like to wield power over others – however low-key – are often found to be lacking in confidence themselves. We see this frequently in adults, too: how often have you come across overbearing, domineering managers ruling by intimidation?

Talk to your child about how he sees himself. You can do this in fairly abstract terms: for example, by getting him to compare himself to his favourite characters in DVDs or books. Ask him which character he is most like and why. Talk to him about which one he would most like to be, and what qualities these characters have that he feels he lacks. In the same way, you can ask him about how he sees himself in relation to his friends: what qualities does he most admire in them? Why does he like being their friend? What does he think they most like about him? By doing this you should be able to begin to build a picture of how high (or low) his self-esteem is. As a parent, you should let your child know that you feel uneasy about his behaviour, and

see if he seems surprised by what you say you've observed. You may be able to head off any further difficult behaviour before it takes hold simply by letting your child know that you are aware of it already.

Another common phenomenon is where the youngest child in a family will play the role of 'big brother' to his friends. This is like the 'pecking order' of the animal world, where the most established creature will be 'top dog' and demand deference from those below him: if he has older siblings, your child may be passing down the line the treatment he gets from them. Middle children from families where the younger sibling is treated as the baby may also adopt this behaviour outside of the family because they know they won't get away with being overly bossy at home.

In all of the above situations, your child may simply be craving more attention and more responsibility at home. If he can feel equal to his other siblings in as many ways as possible, this will boost his self-esteem. If he is an only child, it may be that he yearns to be treated differently, depending on how secure he is feeling – as a big boy sometimes and a baby at others, for example – and you can take your lead from him. Don't be afraid to indulge his occasional regressions, even though he is 11. This is a time of great change as he makes the transition from junior school to high school and he will be expected to act maturely and responsibly throughout the school day; it's hardly surprising then if he wants to retreat occasionally to the relative comfort and safety of his younger days.

It could be, of course, that your child is not suffering from a lack of confidence but is simply naturally protective. In this case, what you are interpreting as bossiness and showing off is in fact his own interpretation of 'parenting' his peers. It could also be that these less assertive children are drawn to him because he appears to them to be more mature and in control.

Most importantly, if his friends seem perfectly happy in his company, then there is probably little to worry about; if you feel the children your son is playing with are finding it hard to assert themselves, perhaps you could intervene just to ensure that they have a say or a turn in their games – and gently remind your son to do the same. If he does appear to be 'showing off', remove him from the limelight temporarily by engaging all the children in a group activity which doesn't require a leader!

My eight-year-old daughter is missing out on social opportunities because she won't try anything new – such as bowling, swimming or ice skating. She will even turn down invitations to parties which include these activities, and as a result she's frequently left off her friends' guest lists. How can I encourage her to be more adventurous?

It's difficult when a child is fearful of new experiences, and it's very likely that a lack of confidence is key to her attitude. Has your child experienced failure in the past when she's tried something new? Perhaps you can

track her reluctance back to a particular incident where she has found herself humiliated, and as a result her personal survival instinct is telling her not to take any more risks.

One way to counteract reticent behaviour is to engender a home life where it's perfectly normal and acceptable to take the odd risk. This doesn't have to involve danger of any kind – it could be that you risk being laughed at, for example. So if your child is good at a particular thing – whether she's a genius at Nintendo, a diva on her dancemat or a master at Swingball – have a go yourself, even if you suspect it won't be your own forte. The point is to show her that it's exciting and adventurous to take risks sometimes, and that failure is all part of learning. Let her see you really enjoying taking part, whether you're any good or not, and tell her afterwards how much fun you had trying.

If the areas she's reluctant to try are mostly sport-driven, it may be that she just doesn't feel proficient enough. Most children are only reluctant to swim, for instance, if they are not competent or don't feel safe in the water. In this case, it's worth signing her up for a course of lessons, even if you or her school have already taught her the basics: it may be that she knows her peers are much stronger or better swimmers than she is, and that she fears she'll be ridiculed if she can't join in with their water play. Take every opportunity to build her confidence: visit your local pool with her (you can take her into the teaching pool if she's very nervous) and just play in the water together; if you have a beach- or pool-based holiday during the year, encourage her to at least get into the water with an inflat-able support, such as a lilo or dinghy, even if she doesn't want to do any more than that. As her confidence builds, show her how to tread water or jump in. She might enjoy water parks where there are non-swimming activities on offer, such as water slides and flumes – you could find that she's simply embarrassed to be seen doing her strokes.

If your child tires easily during games which require her to run around, build her stamina with interesting 'I-Spy' walks: give her a list of things to spot and tick off en route. You can then build up to short games of football or other ball games – but don't push her until she's exhausted, as she will be reluctant to try again. The aim is for her to begin to enjoy more physical pursuits, but taking little steps to fit-ness and competence will pay better dividends than trying to shame her into strenuous exercise. As her confidence grows, you may find that she gradually becomes willing to try something more adventurous, but if she's fearful of hurting herself, don't push her into ice skating, trampolining or other activities which carry a risk of falling.

Finally, acknowledge that we are not all driven by physi-cal pursuits: as long as she is exercising enough to stay healthy – and this could just mean walking to and from school or dancing to her favourite music – you need to accept that her interests may lie in more cerebral pastimes. Meanwhile, have a word with her friends' parents and explain that she is very happy to accept invitations that don't involve this type of sporty activity, and this way she should

find herself back on some of the invitation lists. You can, of course, always organize the odd weekend afternoon play session at home for her friends, and plan her own birthday parties with gentler themes.

Q My six-year-old son seems to have virtually no friends. Although he does get invited to parties, he rarely gets asked back to anyone's house after school, and he never mentions any particular children when he talks about his day. There aren't many children his age in our neighbourhood, so he doesn't get lots of opportunities to strike up friendships locally. He has a brother of eight and a sister of 10 who he gets on well with, and he doesn't seem sad or lonely, but I'm worried that he isn't getting the benefit of friendships. How can I help him?

A The fact that your son does get asked to parties and is invited back to his schoolmates' homes – even if only occasionally – is encouraging; it seems that he is simply happy in himself and doesn't need special friendships for support just yet. At six, he is still quite young for making very close associations, especially as boys tend to take longer than girls to form 'best' friendships.

The fact that he doesn't mention specific children when he's telling you about his day is probably all part of the natural inclination many children have to 'switch off' about school once they get back home. Many parents have to virtually prise the tiniest shred of information out of their children this age – plenty of whom will claim to have forgotten what they did during the course of the day the minute they have left the classroom!

If your son interacts well with his siblings and seems happy and outgoing in himself, I don't think you have much to worry about. He sounds as if he is enjoying the company of the children around him without having become dependent upon them to any extent. If you want to offer him more opportunities to make friends locally, why not see if he would like to join a Beavers group or a regular club at the local leisure centre with same-age children? A mixed group may prove fruitful, as it could be that he finds the boys at school a bit 'full on' but is reluctant to try to befriend the girls there for fear of ridicule. If he takes up an activity which includes girls as well as boys – a swimming club, for instance – he will be able to make friends of both sexes without risking getting teased.

If you want a clearer insight into how other children perceive and interact with your son at school, however, make an appointment to discuss this with his teacher. Primary school staff tend to have a great insight into each child and will be able to describe the way in which he functions socially. You may want to ask whether your child seems to be included in any group activities in the playground; whether he appears to have made friends; whether he does anything that might put other children off befriending him and whether you have any cause to worry. My bet is that you'll get positive feedback to put your mind at rest.

Finally, it may be helpful for you to stand back and think about why you are worried about your son: is it because your child is upset, or is it because you feel that the way your child is treated reflects badly on you? Making sure that we don't become overly involved in our children's struggles is key if they are to develop their own identities and resilience.

Resources

www.babycentre.co.uk

Babycentre offers sensible advice covering pregnancy, babies and toddlers up to 3 years old.

www.bbc.co.uk/parenting

The BBC website provides comprehensive advice and information for parents, and links to further resources.

www.bullying.co.uk

Bullying Online is the UK's leading anti-bullying charity which provides support and advice online for children, their families, schools and youth organizations.

www.childline.org.uk

Tel: 0800 1111
ChildLine is the UK's free, 24-hour helpline that children and young people can call when in distress or danger.

www.kidscape.org.uk

Helpline: 08451 205 204
A charity committed to preventing bullying and sexual abuse of children. It works UK-wide offering advice and support to individuals and organizations on how to keep children safe. They offer a telephone helpline, advice and various literature on how to deal with bullying and abuse.

www.netmums.co.uk

The netmums website offers information for parents and children on a national and local level. You just need to register to gain access to details of local resources such as child-friendly cafes, baby and toddler classes, places to take your children as well as information about child-minders or local schools and nursery places.

www.parentcentre.gov.uk

Tel: 0870 000 2288 (DfES HQ)
Provides helpful information for parents of children of all ages, while offering parent-to-parent and expert-to-parent support via the internet chat forums. It is part of the official Department for Education & Skills (DfES) website.

www.parentlineplus.org.uk

Freephone: 0808 800 2222
Available 24 hours, seven days
a week, ParentlinePlus is a free
and confidential Parentline
staffed by trained volunteers
who offer information and
support, and the chance for
parents to talk to someone
about the issues they are facing.

www.raisingkids.co.uk

Tel: 0208 883 8621
A website for parents of children
of all ages, providing expert
parenting advice, parenting
news and information, and
suggestions for fun family
activities.

www.surestart.gov.uk

Tel: 0870 0002288
Sure Start is a government
programme designed to help
every child have the best start
in life. The website gives
information about early years
education, childcare, health, tax
credits and family support.

www.tinytalk.co.uk

Tel: 0870 2424 898
Tiny Talk run baby sign language
courses all over the country,
which aim to help your baby or
toddler to articulate their needs
before they can speak properly.

Log on to their website or phone
the helpline to find information
on where your nearest class is.

Books

The Antecedents of Self-Esteem,
Stanley Coopersmith
(W.H. Freeman and Co Ltd.)
Pumpkin Soup, Helen Cooper
(Corgi Children's Books)
Water Bugs & Dragonflies,
Doris Stickney
(Continuum Books)